DISCOURSE
AND
DESTRUCTION

The City of Philadelphia
versus MOVE

ROBIN WAGNER-PACIFICI

The University of Chicago Press
Chicago and London

ROBIN WAGNER-PACIFICI is an associate professor of sociology and anthropology at Swarthmore College.

The University of Chicago Press, Chicago 60637
The University of Chicago Press, Ltd., London
© 1994 by The University of Chicago
All rights reserved. Published 1994
Printed in the United States of America

03 02 01 00 99 98 97 96 95 94   1 2 3 4 5

ISBN: 0-226-86976-8 (cloth)
       0-226-86977-6 (paper)

Library of Congress Cataloging in Publication Data

Wagner-Pacifici, Robin Erica.
    Discourse and destruction : the city of Philadelphia versus MOVE /
Robin Wagner-Pacifici.
        p.   cm.
    Includes bibliographical references and index.
(pbk. : alk. paper)
    1. MOVE (Organization)   2. Violence—Pennsylvania—
Philadelphia.   3. Philadelphia (Pa.)—Race relations.
4. Afro-Americans—Pennsylvania—Philadelphia.   5. Black
nationalism—Pennsylvania—Philadelphia.   I. Title.
F158.9.N4W34   1994
305.8'00974811—dc20   93-23835
                                                          CIP

⊗ The paper used in this publication meets the minimum
requirements of the American National Standard for Information
Sciences—Permanence of Paper for Printed Library Materials, ANSI
Z39.48-1984.

DISCOURSE AND DESTRUCTION

To my parents, with love

CONTENTS

PREFACE

In the spring of 1992 the ultimate elemental and symbolic weapon, fire, burned out of control once again in an American city, this time Los Angeles. For Americans old enough to remember the sixties, the image of neighborhoods burning up was all too reminiscent. For those of us who live in and near Philadelphia, the memory was much more recent and raw. That burning in Los Angeles, along with charges of police engaging in both excessive force and excessive inaction, along with the difficulties of a black mayor dealing with a white police commissioner, along with issues of misfired judicial encounters, raised for us the specter of the 1985 MOVE disaster. In that conflict these same elements, reconfigured to the particular contours of Philadelphia's police, its community, its political and racial histories, and the history of the MOVE group, led to the deaths of eleven people (including five children) and the total destruction of a neighborhood by fire burning out of control.

Further, as in Los Angeles, in 1985 precipitating events and actions led to the disaster. Lawmakers, politicians, MOVE members, law enforcers, neighborhood residents, and fire fighters all participated in the lurching march toward confrontation. But if one were asked what the conflict was about, one would be hard-pressed to answer with ease or confidence. Perhaps the conflict was about several things simultaneously: class conflict, racial conflict, religious fervor, political orthodoxy, hygiene, cooking, and language. And perhaps the resultant conflagration was about the utter insufficiency of an essentially legal language and system to grasp a reality that is so socially and morally vexed.

This study is about the relationships among discourse, social power, conflict, and violence. But the MOVE conflict is not simply an occasion for considering these issues. The conflict and the tragic conclusions remain like a thorn in the historical body of the City of Philadelphia. It simply cannot, and should not, be absorbed. In a certain universal sense, the group calling itself MOVE, from the early 1970s up to the current day, has acted like a vortex into which have flowed all of modern civilization's troubles. This study catalogs those troubles, as the various participants in the tragedy and its inquisitional aftermath awkwardly attempted to talk about the normal and the abnormal, the good and the bad, to align their visions of such ideals and their opposites with a very messy reality. MOVE itself has recently proclaimed that the "system" "IS THE CAUSE OF ALL [people's] PROBLEMS (ALCOHOLISM, DRUG ADDICTION, UNEMPLOYMENT, WIFE ABUSE, CHILD PORNOGRAPHY, EVERY PROBLEM IN THE WORLD)" (*Twenty Years on the MOVE*, p. 2). We must hear in the pathos of "every problem in the world," capitalized in the usual MOVE fashion, the echoes of the deaths from 1985. But taking on every problem in the world has always brought trouble, as the rules, norms, habits, laws, and institutions are, in the best of cases, intractable to total overhaul. And then, MOVE had problems of its own—perhaps not the same ones as the society that it confronted, but problems nonetheless. This book charts these problems and positions via attention to the languages that configured them through and beyond the 1985 conflict.

Looking back, nobody believes that the MOVE conflict was handled well (although, in a bizarre moment of foreshadowing, Darryl Gates, Los Angeles police chief, apparently wrote to Mayor Wilson Goode immediately after the confrontation, congratulating him for a job well done). A Special Investigation Commission and two grand juries have yet to bring any individual, institution, or process to justice.

On the one hand, the MOVE conflict was a strange hybrid, a charged space at the intersection of race, modernity, class, nature, urban life, and culture. On the other hand, the MOVE conflict can be viewed as one of a series of cases in which minority groups are confronted head on by the state and its arsenal (and this either in the state's role of friend, as it claimed to be for the neighbors of MOVE, or as its enemy). Recognizing the usual destructive trajectories of frontal assaults—either real or analytical—this study attempts to get at the MOVE conflict and, by analogy, others like it, obliquely. Its claim is that language matters, that it is three-dimensional, containing and sustaining the world toward which language is continually gesturing. If this book has succeeded in its aims, it has done so by jumping into the small cracks between discourse and violence and exploring that critical, if elusive, territory.

ACKNOWLEDGMENTS

Thanks are owed to a number of people and organizations who assisted my thinking and writing over the long haul toward completion. William Brown III provided me with access to all of the Philadelphia Special Investigation Commission files and particularly to the transcripts of the commission's public hearings. William Meeks of the American Friends Service Committee provided me with transcripts from the AFSC Community Outreach section's symposium on the MOVE tragedy and has kept me informed about continuing efforts to understand and memorialize this event and to prevent future such events in Philadelphia. Jack Greene, Jack Nagel, Sue Wells, and Marc Ross have shared papers and insights about the MOVE organization, Philadelphia police, conflict resolution, rhetoric, and city administrations. I thank Marc Ross for lending me his video tapes of the MOVE hearings. Heidi Feldman, Liz Logue, and Amy Barker all helped to gather and analyze data. Their perceptive readings of transcripts and other material gave me much to think about. Kate Cleland, social science reference librarian at Swarthmore College, did a number of computer searches for this project. Friends and colleagues have responded with interest and perceptive comments when asked to read pieces of this book or listen to talks from it. Thus special thanks go to Nathalie Anderson, Harold Bershady, Abbe Blum, Perry Chang, Joy Charlton, Carol Cohn, Jeff Goldfarb, Wendy Griswold, Arlie Hochschild, Mary Poovey, Richard Rubenstein, Magali Sarfatti-Larson, and Barry Schwartz. Doug Mitchell has once again been an astute and enthusiastic editor. Sometimes I think that reading his letters are the best part of this process.

And, of course, there is that wonderful family of mine. I know that thanks are certainly in order for my husband, Maurizio. He dealt single-handedly with the three young Pacificis during those moments I needed for concentration and calm. He is also genuinely interested in my work, which for a biologist is quite a stretch. This interest is extremely sustaining, and I love him for this as for many other things. And as to those three Pacificis mentioned above, Adriano, Laura, and Stefano, I'm not sure they should exactly be thanked. But I am sure that I adore them, and I figure this is as good a place as any to say that.

This research was supported by a grant from the Fund for Research on Dispute Resolution. The opinions expressed herein do not necessarily reflect the position of the fund. This project was also supported by a Eugene Lang Faculty Fellowship grant from Swarthmore College.

CHAPTER ONE

A Framework for Articulating Horror

Over the years I have been analytically attracted to violence. This is perplexing to me, but there it is. This study of the MOVE–City of Philadelphia confrontation is no different. Violence resides at its heart–the violence of a modern city government, the violence of a modern police force, and the violence of a group that pitted itself against what it termed the "system." But as awesome, horrifying, and real as it is, I have found no unmediated way to approach violence, because violence is always mediated by and intertwined with symbolic systems of meaning, particularly language.

Thus this book focuses on the relationship(s) between violence and language in contemporary social life. It interrogates those relationships to see if they can actually be mapped. It asks, Does violence get talked into life? If so, how? Do different discourses talk violence differently, making specific acts of violence more or less palatable, more or less comprehensible? Do certain discourses open themselves up to violence and others make it less feasible? Beyond the specific focus on violence itself, this study aims at exploring the relationships between various ways of talking and ways of seeing. Are there particular discourses of power spoken only by those with the imprimaturs of an institution behind them? And do these institutions themselves generate these discourses from within their established worldviews? Further, do these discourses of the powerful simply suppress the discourses of the deinstitutionalized or the anti-institutional—society's marginal or massive populations? Or do they import elements from the deinstitutionalized discourses—representative images, referential codes, suggestive metaphors, or alternative syntax—that either covertly coopt these subordinate discourses or unconsciously leak them during moments of discursive entropy?

This introduction provides an analytic context for these concerns and questions. It presents the theoretical assumptions and the methodological means for doing discourse analysis. It explains as well the intrinsic and analytical importance of the case of MOVE. The unalterable reality of death and destruction at the center of this study I will not prevaricate or theorize away. My own language will get complicated at times, but remember that it is only a few steps away from the horror. This is precisely the predicament under exploration here—how is horror to be articulated and how is articulation (the process of theorizing or making an academic study about something) horrified?[1]

In order to get at this predicament, I use the tool of discourse analysis. Discourse analysis is a means of gauging worldviews and power relations, as specific decisions and actions are construed and effected over the course of a social crisis. Thus its first analytical target is the (variable) construction of social meaning in social action. The second intellectual burden borne by discourse analysis is the exploration of the contemporary construction of subjectivity and agency. This involves aspects of the poststructuralist problematization of a unified, autonomous, self-contained subject who surveys a world from a vantage point outside of it. Violence is a particularly apt issue for thinking about the problem of the self, for violence always indicates some kind of rupture and transgression of the body, that vital home for the self. Anything that breaks even an imaginary unity could be extremely revealing of the posited boundaries of that unity. All of this is particularly true today, a historical moment of manifold social possibilities and dislocations, when traditional social structures of family, school, state, and so forth find their original foundations evaporating and any new ones transient and relative. Perhaps we may be said now to live permanently in the "shifting and borderline situations" that Gerth and Mills wrote of in *Character and Social Structure*. There they claimed that these situations, "having no stable vocabularies of motive, may contain several alternative sets of motives originally belonging to different systems of roles."[2]

The MOVE conflict brought many of these issues right to the surface as notions of pluralism, life-style, neighborhood, leadership, terror, and law were batted about over the tortuous evolution of the crisis. Discourse analysis can be brought to bear on such a situation, as it is a methodology particularly suited to excavating the patterns of representation of just such concepts. This one complicated case in which language drew to itself the conscious and unconscious attention of all of the participants is well suited for this form of analysis. It provides a context for an analysis that Mary Louise Pratt describes as "focused on modes and zones of contact between dominant and dominated groups, between persons of different and multiple identities, speakers of different languages, that focused on how such speakers constitute each other relationally and in difference, how they enact differences in language."[3]

Further, and in related fashion, I want to make a case for the doing of case studies. Case studies have the benefit of at least starting with some real swatch of human interaction in time and space. Certainly, as Ricoeur and other theorists of the relation between time and narrative have taught us, we the readers, listeners, even the participants, bracket beginnings and ends and call what resides inside a "case" or an "event" or a "historical epoch." Still, all but the most diehard poststructuralists would agree that there is some material grounding, some case out there, that the case study can interrogate. In this, case studies have an advantage over works of pure theory or pure methodology. One might say that they have a certain intrinsic claim on a researcher's mind. In a similar vein, Erving Goffman once wrote that "methodological self-consciousness that is full, immediate and persistent sets aside all study and analysis except that of the reflexive problem itself, thereby displacing fields of inquiry instead of contributing to them."[4] The intent here is to contribute, not to displace.

Case studies also look at concentrated moments of such sociological issues as interaction, organization, and power. They allow for a Geertzian "thick description" that, if done well, will clearly find the macro in the micro. Better yet, case studies demand a kind of permanent state of tacking back and forth between the micro and the macro, the empirical and the theoretical, the one level always suggesting and problematizing the other.

In fact, one might refer to a case study such as the MOVE confrontation as residing at a kind of "midro" level of analysis. This level has significance beyond the temporal and spatial parameters, beyond the plotting of the duration of the object of analysis. It calls forth the issue of how to gauge the appropriate questions to be asked of the case and the appropriate theories and methodologies to be used. In this regard it is important first to say something about the difference between this study and most of those studies of talk-in-action that go under the heading of conversation analysis.

Conversation analysts have addressed themselves to such universal issues as question-answer sequencing in conversation, expectations for appropriate turn-taking responsibilities of participants in a speech situation, the role of insertion sequences, and the rules of co-occurrence.[5] As such, their studies have not, in the large majority of the cases, posed questions about the relationship between talk and power,[6] focusing instead on "elucidating the mechanisms of sequential organization of interaction, that is, the way participants construct their interaction turn by turn over its course to accomplish an accountably coherent exchange."[7] But the relationship between talk and power is at the heart of this study. According to the approach developed here (explained at length below), social discourses both reflect and reproduce power relations that "live" in social structures. These structures can alternatively be described as institutions, a traditional sociological term, or disciplines, a term deriving largely from Foucault's analyses of power. Importantly, the discourses do their work regardless of how attuned or oblivious a given social speaker is to the specific institutional variables of power in each case. By contrast, conversation analysts pin much on speaker orientation, where "professional characterizations of the participants [are] grounded in aspects of what is going on that are demonstrably relevant to the participants, and at that moment."[8]

This notion of demonstrable relevance is so restrictive as to implicitly deny any reality to an unconscious, individual or social in nature, that can impinge upon contextuated talk-in-action in ways that participants may not realize. By contrast, I believe that the macro infuses the micro in lived contexts of interaction. It is the analyst's responsibility to bring his or her understanding of the discursive repertoire of given institutions or disciplines to bear in analyzing the dynamics of talk if, as I preliminarily noted above, the questions the analyst wishes to ask are those that engage issues of power, authority, and violence. The midrolevel of interaction, of which inquisitional hearings such as the MOVE commission hearings represent an instance, seems particularly apt for gauging such issues. There are just enough speaker-to-speaker situated talk and just enough institutional prerogatives and actions at stake to engage the most salient analytic questions of power.

Given this, however, on specific occasions a speaker may self-consciously break out of a given discursive repertoire in order to call attention to the apparently monolithic rules of talk that are systematically being accomplished by fellow participants. This act could be viewed as constituting a violation of the rules of talk. And such a disjunction could indeed be crucial, as it embodies an attempt to signify and challenge the extant authority structures as they are reflected and accomplished in talk. Several such disjunctions occur over the course of the two-month-long MOVE commission hearings, which provide a key source of discursive data for this study. I will analyze such moments in the context of the central chapters' detailing of the several discourses that were at play in this political and social crisis.

What Is Discourse Analysis?

Diverse scholars refer to discourse and discourse analysis in their works. There is enough variability and disagreement over what constitutes discourse and how best to appropriate it for research purposes that I need to clarify the ways in which I am using these terms.

At its most basic level, discourse analysis assumes an important relationship between systems of symbolic representation (most notably speech) and the organizations and institutions of the social world through which such symbol systems flow. It assumes, as Barry Schwartz and I have written elsewhere, that "specific worldviews inhere in the specialized discourses of social organizations . . . These worldviews involve ideas of what it is to be a human being in society and how human beings ought to be represented. Discourse analysis moves back and forth between organizations and the contours of their worldviews by attending to the specific words and acts of organizational incumbents."[9]

From the most minute lexical features of a given speech act to the most overarching of allegorical figures brought to bear in communication and interaction, discourse analysis can trace the representational tendencies. Perhaps the first, and certainly one of the most original and important of discourse analysts, was the literary theorist Mikhail Bakhtin. While centrally concerned with works of literature, notably those of Rabelais, Bakhtin made fruitful analyses of the discourses of social life. He identified the discourses of the student, the doctor, the military cadet as all tending in specific directions in terms of worldviews and interactions: "There is no such thing as an absolutely neutral utterance. The speaker's evaluative attitude toward the subject of his speech (regardless of what his subject may be) also determines the choice of lexical, grammatical and compositional means of the utterance."[10] Thus it is both possible and necessary to work analytically within two levels at once, that of the "evaluative attitude" (what I call worldview here) and that of the so-called linguistic features of speech. One can be read in the other.

The substance of discourse analysis has been variously configured by different scholars. Michel Foucault identifies discourses with the "disciplines" of modern life. These disciplines include such things as medicine, psychiatry, and criminology. The very notion of the human agent varies across these disciplines according to their paradigmatic worldviews. The discipline of psychiatry, for example, holds a central notion of sanity, from which flows specific modes of assessing, naming, and treating human beings as either sane or sick. Foucault terms such disciplinary practice the "power/knowledge nexus" and elaborates in his writings on the way in which power and knowledge are intimately intertwined.

Long before Foucault, Kenneth Burke also concerned himself with differentially configured terms for ultimate motives for human action. He called these "God-terms" and referred to such grounding and motivating notions (the unconscious for Freud, for example) to analyze whole works of art and science. Burke and Foucault are not often thought of as similar in their approaches to social and historical institutions. But in Burke's stress on the way that God-terms infuse and contour all of the conceptions and actions of a given work, I believe there is indeed an essential similarity between the two.

In terms of the way that identifying a God-term might actually function in analyzing an occasion of discourse, Burke gives a clue in a discussion of the analytic ramifications of understanding human agents as relating to, say, a supernatural God (rather than to nature, the unconscious instincts, the means of production, etc.). "If we locate the human agent and his act in terms of a scene whose orbit is broad enough to include the concept of a supernatural Creator, we get a different kind of definition than if our location were confined to a narrower circumference that eliminated reference to the 'supernatural' as a motivating element in the scene, and did not permit the scenic scope to extend beyond the outer limits of nature."[11]

I take Burke to be saying that all discourse is "motivated" in the sense that it harbors an ultimate God-term (acknowledged or not), and, as such, individual discourses have repertoires of the "sayable." It is one of the tasks of this study to chart those contours of sayability as diverse discourses seek to appropriate an event for purposes of control, legitimation, and archivization.

Once one has identified a particular discourse, how does one go about analyzing its social lives? A contemporary writer, Peter Goodrich, uses the term *discursive formation* to refer to the "relation of bodies of knowledge to social practice and structure." He goes on to delineate three levels of discursive formations that are distinctly available for analysis: "those of its material basis, or institutionalization, its self-articulation or internal ordering, intradiscourse, and its relation to other discourses and discursive formations, its interdiscourse."[12] I find this a very useful analytic paradigm. It identifies the multifold lives of discourses as they are spoken into life in institutional settings, as they have internal constraints on their "logic," and as they confront, intermingle, or resist other discourses. For example, to identify and analyze bureaucratic discourse, one would have to look at the institutional modes and structures that construe the bureaucratic discourse and, in a linguistically detailed manner, at that discourse that construes the modes and structures of bureaucratic institutions. Finally, one would have to analyze the interactions of bureaucratic speech with other discourses, say that of religion or psychology. The point is that each level of discursive formations has emergent patterns of articulation. And the greater point is that these patterns have a bearing (however conditional) on what actions can and will be taken.

Discourse Analysis and Material Effects

The question of the material effects of the dominance (or subordinance) of particular discursive formations is both important and ultimately elusive. Some theorists have less ambivalence than I on this issue. Terry Eagleton, for example, characterizes discourse theory as "devoted to analyzing the material effects of particular uses of language in particular social conjunctures."[13] Language, then, is seen to cause certain material effects. I prefer a formulation that is both less causally certain and less apparently linear. In this I agree, with qualification, with the perspectives of Carol Cohn and Wendy Hollway. Hollway writes that "discourses make available positions for subjects to take up."[14] And Cohn's reading of the relationship between discourses and material effects is that discourses create perceptions and thus make certain actions thinkable and possible and others not.[15] Both of these perspectives create an image of contours and boundaries around actions that emerge from a discursive surround, rather than an image of a direct causal relationship between a distinct world of language and a distinct world of action.

My qualification of these perspectives involves discursive counterworlds, worlds in which the institutional discourses have only a fictional relationship to the actions taken by those institutions. And in fact, the discourse and the physical actions proceed in opposite directions. Hannah Arendt brilliantly analyzed such fictional worlds in her study of the institutions and movements of totalitarianism. The fact that the relationship is obverse, however, doesn't mean that there is no relationship. Even here, the discourse is doing something—masquerading, fictionalizing the real actions of those in power—toward effecting the world.

Inter- and Intradiscourse

Assumptions about those aspects of discursive formations that address internal and interactive patterns, constraints, and opportunities vary. Of intradiscursive features Bakhtin writes: "We learn to cast our speech in generic forms and when hearing others' speech, we guess its genre from the very first words; we predict a certain length . . . and a certain compositional structure; we foresee the end; that is, from the very beginning we have a sense of the speech whole, which is only differentiated during the speech process."[16] Here the implication is that each discourse has a set internal structure, recognizable and all of a piece. Alternatively, Robert Sanders stresses the need for a continuous extrinsic process of finding the internal coherence in a given chunk of discourse: "Grounds of coherence are construed in a collection of statements on the expectation that generally results from the existence of some extrinsic connection among those statements (e.g., they are produced by a single source contiguously; they are arrayed on the pages of a single publication . . .). In that case, grounds of coherence, as constructions (rather than artifacts), must be considered fluid and contingent (subject to change over time.)"[17] Here grounded theory can best provide an empirically contextuated solution to this dilemma of how internally set or how internally fluid given discourses actually are. Only by interpreting a given discourse in the light of a given theory of social organization, gender relations, class conflict, and so forth, can the structural (e.g., allegorical, compositional, stylistic, grammatical, lexical) elements of that discourse be charted.

On the specific issue of coherence, I make a case for an alternative view on the internal fixity and insularity of given discourses. The view I espouse is one of discourse contamination. No one discourse can stand on its own; it will always be partial in the eyes of the differentiated audiences of the modern world. Thus an analyst will inevitably find alien images, stylistic flourishes, unanticipated lexical features, and so forth embedded within a given discourse that promises an intact, whole-cloth worldview. It is one of the burdens of this study to identify and interpret such moments of discursive contamination as participants in the MOVE conflict prescribe, enact, and ultimately explain their actions within their specific institutional discourses.

In terms of the way that cotemporaneous discourses interrelate, some theorists speak of a discursive hierarchy (Simon Dentith), while others stress the competing aspects of coextensive discourses (Wendy

Hollway). This distinction, the latter implying more freedom of movement between discourses for the speaking subject, raises the question of individual initiative and intentionality. The idea that people take positions in one or another discourse (thereby constructing their identity within that ideological, political, or institutional alignment) rather than simply being predetermined either by the dominant discourse's dominance or by something like a material basis of class, race, gender, and so forth, entails a notion of at least partially free agency. Even those, like Hollway, who posit an active agency qualify such activity by writing of a "power" that has been inscribed in a person's subjectivity: "By claiming that people have investments . . . in taking up certain positions in discourses, and consequently in relation to each other, I mean that there will be some satisfaction or pay-off or reward . . . I theorize the reason for this investment in terms of power and the way it is historically inserted into an individual's subjectivity."[18]

Thus even an active agency moving about among competing discursive formations is already necessarily a subject of discourses of power. In order to excavate that power, some concept of interpretation must be posited (the interpreter somehow being able to stand outside the extant hierarchical or competing discourses in order to turn them inside out).[19] Further, as Jameson writes, that concept of interpretation "always presupposes, if not a conception of the unconscious itself, then at least some mechanism of mystification or repression in terms of which it would make sense to seek a latent meaning behind a manifest one, or to rewrite the surface categories of a text in the stronger language of a more fundamental interpretive code."[20]

With his primary orientation of Marxism, Jameson's chosen master code (or Burkean God-term) is that of class conflict. My analytic and empirical distrust of metanarratives moves me alternatively to suggest a series of master codes that emerge and recede in different discursive formations. Thus in the MOVE conflict one might identify the class nature of the conflict between MOVE (antitechnology, antisystem) and its neighbors on Osage Avenue (upwardly mobile, mainstream); or one might focus on the situational disenfranchisement of black political leaders unhinged from their power and authority in crises by their white subordinates; or one might reveal unconscious struggles with the superego as political bureaucrats obsessively and unsuccessfully fixate on control. I do not believe that it is possible or necessary to choose one or the other code as "master" in order to interrogate the meaning of an event. In fact, I am interested precisely in the contaminations and combinations of such interpretive codes in actual moments of social discourse. Both the possibilities for change and the constraints on change are made most visible in such interstitial moments.

The Question of Intentionality

The notion of active, free, speaking agents picking and choosing strategically among social discourses must be highly qualified. This qualification must be outlined despite Bakhtin's optimism about the possibility of one's own voice "liberating itself from the authority of the other's discourse."[21] Here I highlight two ways in which such choices are qualified.

The first constraint involves the availability of discourses at any given time and in any given institutional context. Thus a bureaucrat ought normally to sound like a bureaucrat and not a mystic. This constraint, going back to the idea of contamination, is not absolute. In another context Wendy Griswold writes against the notion of absolute fixity of cultural genres (analogous here to discursive formations).[22] Genres do undergo transformations: coherence will continue to be read by an audience faced with a genre mottled by the process of change. Even a bureaucrat can articulate images of a sentimental nature, as we shall see, and the discourse, institutional setting, and incumbent will all continue to be read as bureaucratic. Discursive change is ultimately limited, however. The limits must be charted both theoretically and empirically.

The second constraint upon speakers of discourse refers to an extant social demand for both rational and ethical coherence. This demand transcends any particular discursive formation in our contemporary culture. And it is precisely that combination of the rational and the ethical that is so perplexing. For these two ideal-typical worldviews, these two discursive universes cannot be directly acknowledged by each other. Their languages are mutually exclusive. As Isaiah Berlin claimed, in his famous essay on Machiavelli's *Prince*, there are parallel "moral" universes from which to choose. In some ways, our contemporary civilization has raised the ante in its demand for the (impossible) combination of these two ideal-typical universes. We will see the results of such a demand in the linguistic struggles of the protagonists in the MOVE conflict to cobble these universes together.

The City of Philadelphia and the MOVE Conflict

The group calling itself MOVE has been, from its very inception in the early 1970s, difficult to describe. This is partly a result of the multi-issue agenda the group has always stressed and partly a result of a self-conscious resistance to categorization on the part of MOVE members. Group members are insistent, in fact, that the name MOVE itself does not stand for anything. Categorical opaqueness is also the result of the extremely contested nature of the public descriptions of MOVE that have emanated from the City of Philadelphia, from the media, and from MOVE itself. Everything from characterizations of child-rearing practices to the actual causal chronology of historical interactions between MOVE and others, including city administrators, is given contested readings. In most studies the existence of such divergent "records" is cause for much preoccupation about making valid judgments regarding the relative reasonableness of respective stories. The researcher understands the task to be one of sifting through the different stories and excavating evidence for the veracity of one rather than another. Add to that the self-conscious resistance of one of the parties to the very act of self-identification, and the task becomes that much harder. Add to that the poststructuralist suspicion of apparently mimetic descriptions of social life, and the task seems almost impossible.

It is important to clarify that such a task, whatever position one ultimately takes on post-structuralist skepticism, is not the task that I have posed for this study. This study is not, ultimately, about the *what* of MOVE and its stories but about the *how* of them. I wish to investigate, through a discourse analysis, the process by which certain stories came to be told about MOVE, MOVE's neighbors, potential mediators, city officials, police, and others. And I aim to elaborate the real ramifications of the telling of particular stories rather than others. Perhaps this is a way to short-circuit the radical skepticism of the poststructuralists while acknowledging their insights. Rather than attempt to move from competing narratives, each with their own ultimate grounds of motives (God-terms), to the "true" story, I prefer to shift the focus onto the interactions among the discourses in their institutional settings and onto the implications of their descriptions and prescriptions for the lives of real people in crisis.

Given this clarification, I need anyway to provide a description of the scene of the action. What histories of MOVE, of the City of Philadelphia, of Mayor Wilson Goode, of African-Americans in Philadelphia, brought all participants to the day of the tragic confrontation, May 13, 1985?

Philadelphia Racial Politics in the 1970s and 1980s

A large, historic, and once production-oriented city of the Northeast, Philadelphia in the 1970s experienced many of the economic and demographic changes that confronted all comparable big cities in the United States. Production declined; middle-class citizens, both black and white, moved out as the minority racial composition of the city became more pronounced. By 1980 the population of Philadelphia was 52% white, 39% African-American, and 4% Latina/o. Despite these figures, city politics in Philadelphia in the 1970s seemed to go through a period of denial and repression, actually reversing, during the mayoralty of Frank Rizzo, gains that had been made in biracial political coalitions.

According to Richard A. Keiser, during Rizzo's first term (1971–75) "in addition to condoning a policy of police brutality against blacks that ultimately led to a federal investigation of the police force, Mayor Rizzo systematically waged war on the city's black leadership."[23] However, a special city charter revision referendum, spearheaded by Mayor Rizzo to allow him to run beyond the allotted two terms, had by 1979 provoked a resurgence in coalition activity between white liberals and African-Americans in the city. The referendum was defeated, and a new mayor, William Green, appointed an African-American as the city's managing director. This was Wilson Goode.

In many ways, the figure of Wilson Goode is central in this study, and I will draw the contours of his public persona in the context of the chapter on bureaucratic discourse. Here it is important to highlight something about his political trajectory, to understand the political "identikit" he brought to the jobs of managing director and mayor.

The son of southern sharecroppers, Wilson Goode worked his way through Morgan State University on an ROTC scholarship. After college, he served two years in the early 1960s at Fort Carson, Colorado, in the military police division. After leaving the service, he was first a probation officer in Philadelphia and then the housing director of a nonprofit agency called the Philadelphia Council for Community Advancement (PCCA). During this time, Goode went back to school and got an M.A. from the Wharton Business School at the University of Pennsylvania. Called to Harrisburg by Governor Milton Shapp in 1978, Goode took a position on the Public Utilities Commission. His next job was managing director of Philadelphia. These biographical details make it clear that Goode always sought the organizational route to issues of civil rights and social change. He also maintained close ties to the Baptist church, becoming a deacon. His religious faith and affiliation is interesting because Goode understands God to have been dynamically involved in his political life. "The tremendous support of the churches [during his first mayoral campaign] was not an affirmation of my political savvy but another example of God pouring out of his blessings upon me. I had lived for the Lord most of my life through my involvement in the church and my attempt to uphold God's values in the community. Now he was giving back to me tenfold what I had given to him."[24]

As a moderate politician, Goode confronted the challenges that all mayors of large postindustrial cities face. Further, being a member of a minority, he encountered special problems. Albert Karnig and Susan Welch write: "Black mayors and council members have special problems: they must act swiftly to assure the black electorate that they are committed to redressing long-standing grievances, but there are also powerful counter-forces from the white community pressing for only cautious movement."[25]

Into this urban context of social, economic, and political change of the 1970s and 1980s entered a predominantly African-American group of men and women calling itself MOVE.[26]

MOVE

MOVE was founded in the early 1970s in Philadelphia by a sometime handyman named Vincent Leaphart. Together with a graduate student in social work from the University of Pennsylvania, Leaphart (now calling himself John Africa; all MOVE members took the last name of Africa) wrote a tract that laid out his beliefs, called *The Guidelines*. The organization that grew up around John Africa was MOVE. The precise focus of the group was multiplex. From their house/headquarters in the Powelton Village section of West Philadelphia (this neighborhood of racially diverse people with largely single-family dwellings, as well as a few cooperative or communal homes, was adjacent to Drexel University), MOVE members washed cars, walked dogs, and chopped firewood for money. They viewed themselves as a political organization and stressed several basic themes and dicta for MOVE's members. These included animal rights, antitechnology, and vegetarianism. A general antisystem position brought them into conflict with police and the judicial system, as they demonstrated at pet stores, zoos, political rallies, and other public forums, were arrested, and often ended up in court.

MOVE members also confronted society in the ways in which they presented themselves personally. They eschewed middle-class modes of dress (although a number of the members came from middle-class backgrounds and some had been to college) and wore their hair in dreadlocks. Children were considered central figures in the MOVE organization, and the babies did not wear diapers but defecated in the yard along with the animals that MOVE kept. This was all in line with the back-to-nature principle of *The Guidelines*. But it created great tension between MOVE members and the neighbors in Powelton Village, many of whom complained of a great stench coming from the MOVE house and of rats running freely around the house. Diet was also a big part of MOVE's focus. MOVE members ate mainly raw fruits and vegetables and rejected cooked food in general.

In a certain sense, MOVE formed a countersociety to the one in which its members lived. They did not send their children to school, believing that schools, like all extant social and political institutions, were corrupt and enslaving. And they took quite seriously their task of raising *pure* MOVE members, believing that the children, who had not been raised on television and cooked food, were the truest MOVE members. They shared the money that they made from the car wash and other local jobs. They did not pay their utility bills. And then there was their language.

Language is at the heart of this study as well as at the heart of the MOVE confrontation. Thus it is critical to attempt to understand the role of language in the historical development of MOVE. According to MOVE members writing a history of the group, MOVE "strategized profanity to expose the profane circumstances of the system's injustice."[27] Whether the use of profanity in public diatribes against the system was or wasn't originally self-consciously political in the way that MOVE now claims it was, it is clear that it took on a political life of its own as various neighborhoods (Powelton Village, Osage Avenue) and politicians (Rizzo, Goode) focused as much of their energy and concern on MOVE's language as on its alleged hygiene and legal infractions.

Arrests and trials followed MOVE's various confrontations with police during its demonstrations. MOVE members claimed that the police were harassing them, arbitrarily applying disorderly conduct charges whenever they wanted. Indeed, Rizzo's police force had a reputation for violent behavior particularly aimed against minorities. In May 1977, with several MOVE members arrested and convicted of crimes and serving significant jail sentences, others, claiming to be mindful of the government violence against the Black Panthers, staged a demonstration with firearms on the front porch of their house in Powelton Village. Police surveillance intensified at this point and culminated in a blockade that lasted for months. Negotiation attempts failed, including a plan to relocate MOVE to a farm. A shoot-out in August 1978 left one policeman dead, one MOVE member badly beaten by police, and the house bulldozed to the ground. Nine adult members of MOVE were taken into custody. All were charged and convicted of the policeman's death.

Powelton Village was a neighborhood forthrightly diverse in its population and outlook. Liberal white professionals and working-class African-Americans lived together in self-conscious harmony. MOVE pushed against the neighborhood's tolerant self-identity, pushing race and class issues right to the surface. After the show of guns on the porch and the heightened police invasion of the neighborhood, various groups sprang up, expressing diverse positions on the MOVE-city conflict. As well, neighbors articulated a range of conflicts of their own. Life-style and hygiene and smell and language: all of these things accounted for points of possible contention. Yet only a few of the groups were willing to call MOVE "urban terrorists." Most groups, of whom more will be said later, claimed a qualified support for MOVE and expressed a tortured, liberal form of hope for a negotiated settlement. Such was not to be.

One of the most difficult aspects of MOVE's public life is its wavelike quality. There have been periods of relative quiescence during which MOVE is merely a "chronic headache," as one reviewer of this book put it. And then some dynamic develops between MOVE and the city or MOVE and the neighborhood in which it is located, the stakes and behaviors intensify, and MOVE is termed "revolutionary" or "terroristic." So in an important sense the notion of an *evolving* public representation of MOVE is not adequate. Rather, since at least the mid-1970s, MOVE has been viewed intermittently as everything from a nuisance to a terrorist group. The odd and perplexing thing is that so many diverse characterizations continually hover about the group, as if they are in perpetual storage available for moments of crystallization to give a face to the emergent legal, communal, and civil conflicts.

In the early 1980s MOVE members who had not been convicted in the 1978 killing of the police officer set up house in West Philadelphia on a narrow street named Osage Avenue. The street of row houses largely owned by the inhabitants was predominantly African-American. Occupations ranged from teacher to janitor to nurse to policeman. People lived in close quarters, and much of the life of the block took place on the front porches that characterize the homes in West Philadelphia.

During the early 1980s MOVE members lived in relative harmony with their neighbors. The house in which they lived had been owned for many years by an older woman who was a former MOVE member. At least some of those MOVE members living in the house were familiar to the other residents, having grown up in the neighborhood. During these first years MOVE members petitioned the newly elected Mayor Goode to reopen the trial of those convicted in 1978. Goode was willing to meet with them and to listen but ultimately claimed not to have the authority to act on the matter. At this point MOVE began a campaign of provocation against the political leaders by publicly airing the members' complaints over a loudspeaker mounted on their house. Their language was harsh, threatening, and profane. Once again, neighbors of MOVE found themselves wedged between the city and the MOVE organization, both literally, in their houses, and figuratively, in being the targets of MOVE's polemical rhetoric.

After an aborted police action on the sixth anniversary of the 1978 MOVE-city confrontation, MOVE members began fortifying their house with wood, steel, and railroad ties. The house began to resemble a fortress. The neighbors eventually appealed to Goode and other politicians for help. And in the spring of 1985 Goode handed the task of dealing with MOVE over to his managing director, the retired African-American army general Leo Brooks, and to the white police commissioner, Gregor Sambor.

On May 13, 1985, after evacuating the neighborhood and surrounding the MOVE house with five hundred police armed with military and commercial explosives (C-4 and Tovex), automatic and semi-automatic weapons, sharpshooter rifles, two M-60 machine guns, UZIs, shotguns, a silenced .22-caliber rifle, and a Lahti antitank weapon, the police commissioner announced, via a bullhorn, warrants for the arrest of four of the adult MOVE members in the house (a number of children were also living there). The commissioner's ultimatum to vacate the house was rejected by MOVE. At this point, the Philadelphia Fire Department's powerful squirt guns were trained on the house. Police officers fired tear gas and smoke projectiles at the house to provide cover for police insertion teams. An exchange of bullets ensued that lasted, intermittently, until 5:27 P.M. At that point, a police helicopter dropped a satchel of explosives onto the roof of the MOVE house. Minutes later, the pilot reported seeing flames on the roof. After forty minutes, the "squirts" of the fire department were turned on for the first time that evening. By then, the fire was out of control. The fire destroyed the MOVE house and two city blocks of homes. Eleven MOVE adults and children died in the fire.

On May 22, 1985, Wilson Goode issued Executive Order 5-85, announcing the creation of the Philadelphia Special Investigation Commission, composed of eleven private citizens, to "conduct a thorough, independent and impartial examination of the events leading up to and including the incident of May 13, 1985, in the neighborhood of 6221 Osage Avenue in Philadelphia, Pennsylvania."

The MOVE Commission Hearings

This book focuses on two crystallizing moments in this long confrontational history: the days up to and including May 13, 1985, and the weeks of the Philadelphia Special Investigation Commission hearings. It tracks the various participants—MOVE members, neighbors of MOVE, city officials, police, fire fighters, and others—to that day and those hearings. I interrogate these moments and paths with discourse analysis, exploring the discursive surround of the event: the memos from city officials to each other; the minutes of meetings; the letters from the neighbors to politicians; the mass media reports, editorials, and features; the police surveillance sheets; the transcripts of MOVE's loudspeaker speeches; a survey of Philadelphians on the issues of the confrontations, published by the American Friends Service Committee; the transcripts of the 1981 trial of John Africa and the 1985 trial of Ramona Africa, and the videotapes and written transcripts of the MOVE Commission hearings.[28] However, the centerpiece of this study is the languages emergent in the hearings.

The MOVE commission's investigation of the confrontation of May 13 culminated in a series of public hearings, broadcast live over the local public television and radio networks in October 1985. The commission (the members of which were picked by Mayor Goode) was composed of roughly equal numbers of blacks and whites, including six lawyers, one bank executive, three religious leaders, and the president of a community town watch. The two chief questioners for the commission were a former federal prosecutor and a former state prosecutor. There were thirty-six sessions in all. Over ninety witnesses were called. Along with the Big Four (Goode, Brooks, Sambor, and Fire Commissioner William Richmond) neighbors of MOVE, city officials, experts on explosives and fires, two former MOVE members, the one surviving MOVE child, police and fire fighters, and local neighborhood leaders were called. The interactions among various witnesses (while they were almost always insulated from each other in different sessions of the hearings, there was opportunity for cross-referencing previous testimonies) and between witnesses and commissioners reveal a series of discursive moves aimed at historicizing or narrativizing the event. The variety of discourses brought to bear on this project, along with the implicit (if ultimately unrealizable) goal of codifying a master narrative out of the recollections, ideas, and opinions of the witnesses and commissioners makes this context ideal for the kind of linguistic analysis Pratt has described. The hearings thus constituted a (qualified) zone of contact among diverse discourses, some dominant, some submerged. The goal here is to systematically chart those discursive formations as they appear, keeping in mind both their internal and interdiscursive complexity.

Social ruptures such as the MOVE tragedy open up a tear in the social fabric and expose the weave. In fact, ruptures that make problematic a society's vision of itself, by revealing unleashed internal excesses (violence, neglect, and so forth), call forth a series of reparative mechanisms to literally redo the social order. As in surgery, certain connections are made, others may be clamped off, and those people in the operating room get to see how the body is actually put together. In contemporary terms, these mechanisms often involve investigatory commissions, detailed to lay the body/story before the public and then to sew it up. One might analyze the work of these commissions as having several interacting agendas. They do repair work; they attempt to "make sense" of the events, here responding to some greater threat of narrative, epistemological, moral, and/or political heterogeneity; they tend in the direction of locating poles of responsibility (designating blame, praise, and pity); and, finally, they document events. In other words, they create archives, issue reports. I will follow the contributions of both inquisitors and witnesses to this process in the MOVE case. These co-authors may be viewed in a variety of lights.

In their study of the Iran-Contra hearings, Bogen and Lynch write of a twin burden on witnesses testifying in such inquisitional settings: "Responses to investigative questioning will often need to be tailored to the twin demands of providing adequate testimonial evidence while at the same time protecting respondent's position as a teller of and party to the events in question."[29] These conditions indicate a need for witnesses to strategize their testimony. Bogen's and Lynch's study also presupposes and demonstrates that (some) witnesses are able to strategize in such a way that guilt or responsibility is deflected. Throughout this book and particularly in chapter 6, I explore the ramifications of such positionings and repositionings, to gauge which discourses are the best deflectors and which witnesses get to operate with and within those discourses. Although my analytic interests differ slightly from those of Bogen and Lynch, my assumptions about the way witnesses talk in inquisitional settings does not contradict theirs, but rather comes at the testimonies from a different angle. I am assuming that institutional discursive formations have a power to overwhelm contingent situational demands. In other words, even given a felt need on the part of some witnesses both to give evidence and to protect their participant positions, these witnesses do not sound qualitatively different in the hearings than they did throughout the event. The one important qualification of this assumption is that, in those cases in which witnesses actively try to sound different, that difference registers as a kind of unconscious discursive leakage in the testimony.

Finally, let me say a few words about the nature of investigative hearings. The MOVE hearings are of a type generally known as inquisitional procedures, as opposed to adversarial procedures. The general sense is that witnesses are granted a greater degree of freedom in the telling of their stories in the inquisitional setting than in the adversarial. Inquisitional hearings aim overtly at fact-finding and story codifying, rather than at blame and guilt dealing: "Whereas the modern inquisitorial model combines questioning by the judge [in our case, the commission counsel] and relative freedom for witnesses to tell their stories in open-ended narrative style, the adversary model requires tight control of questioning so that claims are generally expressed only as answers to very specific questions."[30] Modern precedents for the MOVE hearings include the Kerner commission hearings, the Violence Commission hearings, the Watergate commission hearings, the Iran-Contra hearings, and the British Widgery hearings.

Inasmuch as the inquisitional model promises greater freedom for witnesses to tell their stories in their own tempos and their own words, divergences from this freedom are interesting and revealing. These accounts receive differential responses, everything from acceptance and narrative support to rejection and narrative exile. As Harvey Molotch and Deirdre Boden demonstrate, the dynamics of power relations are absolutely involved in discursive interactions in these inquisitional settings. In their article about the Watergate hearings, they aim their analysis at exploring "the linkage between power as an attribute of social-structural location and power as a contingent process."[31] They develop an analysis of three faces of power: "The first face of power is the capacity to prevail in explicit contests . . . a second face of power . . . is the ability to set agendas, to determine the issues over which there will be any explicit contest at all . . . Our third face of power is the most basic of all; it is the ability to determine the very grounds of the interactions through which agendas are set and outcomes determined; it is the struggle over the linguistic premises upon which the legitimacy of accounts will be judged."[32]

Molotch and Boden analyze the fates of discursive moves on the parts of pro- and anti-Nixon participants in the Watergate hearings. They locate a point of essentially unresolvable conversational tension in the notion of a White House cover-up and Nixon's knowledge of it. The lack of resolution has to do with John Dean's contested claim that Nixon knew of the cover-up, that claim being contested largely via a counter-claim that the knowledge was "merely" contextuated. Molotch and Boden make clear that the dual, and contradictory, epistemological imperatives of social life decree that knowledge claims ought to be objective and that humans are always engaged in interpretation. This leaves all claims subject to challenge.

In the best of circumstances, that is, when all participants in a speech event are of equal or near-equal power (can engage in the setting of agendas and in the determining of the linguistic premises upon which accounts will be judged), this essential paradox is problematic. But most circumstances are not the best, and contemporary social life is populated by situations of unequal power. Participants in inquisitional hearings, for example, enter as representatives of institutions, as occupants of social roles. Further, following the ethnomethodologists, power must be continually accomplished in situ, as institutions and roles are enacted and embodied, often in speech. The structural determinants of power can be viewed as engaging the interactional determinants of power, and some witnesses gain legitimacy for their narrative forms and/or substance and some do not. The focus of a discourse analysis that gauges the dynamics of enacted power is on the ways in which particular actors build their narratives from within diverse discursive formations. Police, neighbors, city administrators, politicians, lawyers, community activists, firemen, former MOVE members, technical experts, citizens-on-the-street, journalists, and MOVE members all participated in the process whereby discourse diversely configured the reality of the MOVE/city/neighborhood conflict. Here differences of social location (variables of institutional membership, race, education, class, and age in particular) were translated into different discourse repertoires and thus into differential access to the "official story."

In a related study, Brenda Danet focuses on the forms of questions put to different witnesses during the Watergate hearings. Anti-Nixon senators used polite and indirect forms when questioning sympathetic witnesses such as John Dean and used more coercive forms when questioning the recalcitrant such as John Ehrlichman.[33] In the MOVE hearings, it wasn't so much the case that styles of questioning varied from witness to witness as it was that some witness testimonies made it into the final report, the putative master narrative, and some didn't. In other words, what was important was the fate of testimonies in this inquisition, not, as in other inquisitions in history, to indict or vindicate a given witness but to make it or not into the history. However, there must have been enough divergence in question style or in witness reception of questions to elicit the following from one of the former MOVE members who testified. After a series of questions about her contacts with police, this witness said: "Let me say something to you. I get the feeling this is taking on all the aspects of a trial, when in fact it has been publicized, I have heard and read, where this is not a trial. . . And I'm beginning to feel as though Laverne and I are on the witness box."[34]

Thus, at least for some witnesses, something of the historically perfidious sense of the Inquisition lingers even in modern inquisitions.

Overview

Four distinct discursive formations run through and constitute this case. They are (1) the domestic, comprising images of home, family, children, and neighborhood; (2) the bureaucratic, comprising images of policies, hierarchies, plans, memos, agencies, and meetings; (3) the military, comprising images of war, enemies, operations, and tactics; and (4) the legal, comprising images of guilt, crimes, rights, discretions, and warrants. Each substantive chapter in the book tracks the workings out of these discursive formations in the various speech acts (here broadening the notion of speech act to include written texts such as memos) of the participants. Each chapter identifies conflicts over definitions of situations, moments of discursive domination, and moments of discursive interaction and/or contamination. Later chapters cover the territory of earlier chapters, going back over decisions or issues already examined under the lens of a particular discursive formation. But they do so under a different rubric, focusing on different clusters and combinations of clusters of terms for reality.

Chapter 2 looks closely at the question, What is MOVE? This question haunted the city administration of Philadelphia, the neighbors of MOVE on Osage Avenue, the mass media, and the general public. MOVE's history is gauged via a discourse analysis of social constructions of its members' language, their life-style, and their violence. This chapter is broadly chronological in presenting various stories of MOVE's presence in Philadelphia. It considers the characterization of MOVE as a terrorist group, investigating the ramifications of such a determining.

Chapter 3 explores the related languages of domesticity and sentimentality. It focuses on the perceptions and representations of life on the 6200 block of Osage Avenue of those who either lived there or came into official or unofficial contact with it. The notions of family, childhood, and hygiene are all explored, as the MOVE house is juxtaposed against the neighbor houses. In particular, a recurring preoccupation of the MOVE hearings—what a child is—is examined. The deaths of the MOVE children stuck in the center of every narrative of the MOVE confrontation, setting off an obsessive exploration of the MOVE children's status. Were they children, hostages, "hostages," guerrilla fighters, or some unholy combination of the four? Comparisons and contrasts with other neighborhood children were attempted, as the discourse of domesticity collided with discourses of bureaucracy and war. The testimony of the surviving MOVE child, Birdie Africa/Michael Moses Ward, is examined particularly closely for what it can reveal about our contemporary languages of childhood and their vicissitudes.

Chapter 4 establishes the contours and roles of bureaucratic discourse in the MOVE conflict. It first elaborates and calibrates the purview of the bureaucratic discourse in the evolution of this conflict. But it also has an analytic sensitivity to the dependence of even dominant discourses on other discourses. As theories of bureaucracy suggest notions of human agency and human interaction, the persona of the bureaucrat is a central focus of this chapter. The relationship between bureaucracies and a nonbureaucratic world of clients and charges is also evaluated. Such issues as bureaucratic dysfunction, self-splitting, instrumentality, and uncertainty emerge at the heart of the city's approaches to and problems with MOVE. As the policy, plan, and operation that led to May 13 discursively emerged from the background of meetings and memos, several issues of bureaucratic organization came to the surface in the language of the incumbents. Among these, most centrally, were the issues of control and orders. Both proved to be elusive.

Chapter 5 turns to the legal world, in both its interpretive and its violent manifestations. Thus it looks at the languages of lawyers and police in the MOVE conflict as decisions were made about what a crime was, who was guilty, when arrest warrants should be written, and how they should be served. This chapter particularly focuses on charting the relationships between legal documents and decisions and such things as tear gas and explosives, these being relationships that are "normally" submerged in a professionally specialized world. Because the issue of language is at the heart of this study, the variable relationships between speech and crime are examined. When is a threat a threat? When is profanity a civil right? This chapter also looks at the roles of a group of participants that I call "organic mediators." These were local civic and civil rights leaders who attempted, with a different discourse, to provide some grounds for negotiations with MOVE. It is important to situate them between the city lawyers and the city police, a position that they attempted to occupy, with no success, on May 13. Finally, the police operation is examined in terms of the variations on police discourse. The focus is on public and private speech of police as it interacted with the assessments of MOVE's speech. The police presentation of their own violence and violent tools is analyzed via an identification of the two discourses that predominated in these presentations: the discourses of domesticity and of war. This strange coupling is in many ways emblematic of the findings of the whole study.

In chapter 6, I answer some of the questions posed about the relationship of language to violence at the beginning of this introduction. We confront these important questions as citizens of a civilization that claims to have successfully segregated language (laws, conversations, meetings, etc.) from violence. Those points where the differences are muddied, where language can itself be viewed as violence, where violence is sanctioned by a memo or a warrant, are the points of most interest and concern. Further, the (possible and actual) relations of discursive formations to each other in configuring events and determining authority and responsibility are analytically summarized and interpreted. Limits of sayability within given discourses can lead to a variety of speech acts. Here the issues of discourse dependence and contamination come into play. Finally, the horror of the case under analysis insists upon some lesson about the way we talk our way into and out of conflicts. That lesson must refer to the very notions of self that participants in conflicts sustain through their self-presentations. In chapter 6, the various takes on the self that have surfaced in this analysis of the MOVE conflict are pitted against each other for what they allow by way of opportunities for social interaction and for what they prevent. Short of conjuring some discursively ideal self, this is the closest I can come to contributing at all to the prevention of a similar horror in the future.

CHAPTER TWO

What Is MOVE?

Diacrisis (separation) which is the basis of collective and individual identity—responds with visceral, murderous horror, absolute disgust, metaphysical fury, to everything which lies in Plato's hybrid zone; everything that passes understanding, that is, the embodied taxonomy, which by challenging the principles of the incarnate social order . . . violates the mental order, scandalously flouting common sense.

Pierre Bourdieu, *Distinction*

Under normal conditions it would have been unthinkable to mobilize such massive force to evict occupants from a house, but there is nothing normal about MOVE.

Editorial, *Philadelphia Inquirer*, May 14, 1985

I believe that all but the most simple actions are overdetermined. Motives are multiple, conscious and unconscious intertwining in ways that are ultimately, if the analyst is truly honest, unknowable. Some geniuses, Freud and Marx for example, hit upon God-terms, as Kenneth Burke would call them—the unconscious and class conflict—and built enormous theories from them. All would agree on their brilliance, but at the same time, most would agree on their insufficiency.

Thus while the analytic focus here is on the shaping power of language, I do not intend to derive social action from language in a simple causal manner. The relationship is more complicated. When I claim that the degree to which a widespread and persistent preoccupation on the part of the city administrators and the mass media with the *categorical* identity of MOVE led the city to take the actions it finally did, I cannot say that the process is simply one that is causal and linear. I cannot say, for example, that because the police and the district attorney and the mayor had moments in speeches, warrants, and so forth in which they use the term *terrorist* to label MOVE, that that labeling process *caused* the choice of weapons and strategies taken by the police and fire fighters on May 13. However, my guess is that such categorizing (and it was tortuous in its permutations and contradictions) fed into the process of policy formation and strategic and tactical action. This dilemma is the nub of the discourse analysis problematic: How can we characterize the relationships between discourse and action? Perhaps I can only circle around this problem by saying that there must be some relationship or people wouldn't spend so much time and energy talking and writing, gesturing toward the world in symbolic, discursive systems. But I also contend that the relationships are not completely predictable. Countries with fine-sounding constitutions can harbor dictatorial policies. Countries with multiple antiterrorist statutes can be relatively democratic. This does not stop people from worrying about and fighting over wording—of laws, of policies, of petitions, of speeches, of press releases.

In the case of MOVE I contend that the general preoccupation with the question What is MOVE? and the desperate solution of the label *terrorists* by those in a position to act suggests a fierce and grinding relationship between discourse and action.

Let me come clean. I don't know exactly what MOVE was. I don't believe they were terrorists as I have come to understand that term (a term that is none too useful even in more usual contexts).[1] But I would not have been easy with them as neighbors. On the other hand, they were not merely a "nuisance," as one MOVE special investigation commissioner came to use the term. Everything they did, they did to excess, a theme that I will take up centrally. In fact, I believe the whole endeavor to label the group was a dead end and actually a bar to a resolution. But the social minds of human beings press forward the process of identification and categorizing, and when a group like MOVE falls through the categorical cracks, a certain panic arises. I chart the trajectory of that categorical panic in this chapter.

First, I tell *a* story of MOVE so that the reader has some sense of the parameters of time, space, social organization, and social interaction of the group. It's a *story* because it is selective and told in my language. This can't be helped. I use several voices to try to give the same contradictory effect that an actively interested Philadelphia citizen of the midseventies to mideighties might have gotten.

One of the first impressions a reader of the many stories of MOVE has is that there was no smooth development of a public definition of the group. Terms used early on—*radical group, religion,* and *revolutionary group*—came in and out of focus. The label *terrorist* seems to have been used first in 1978 when MOVE members were charged with, among other things (e.g., rioting, failure to disperse, disorderly conduct), "terroristic threats." At that point in time, interestingly, that charge was categorized as a misdemeanor. But even given this prismatic public impression of MOVE, it is possible to say that the group was always represented as contradictory. In this, though not perhaps in the selected emphases on one or another characteristic, this public representation matched MOVE's own self-portrait: "Unlike MOVE, most of the organizations that had participated in the civil rights and antiwar movements and their progeny, had espoused but one or two goals. MOVE juxtaposed so many goals that the resulting mixture became unstable and essentially contradictory. Its adherence to self-defense, for example, conflicted with its admonition to preserve all living things."[2]

In the following pages, I lay out those contradictions by presenting perspectives that emphasize some of the mix of characteristics. As other authors have discovered, it is fruitless to attempt to gauge the rationality or irrationality of the MOVE group.[3] It is not even clear what one gains by claiming the rationality of a group or institution. Does such a label insure responsiveness or predictable actions? As I demonstrate in chapter 4, the hyper–instrumentally rational bureaucracy of the city administration, with all of its preoccupations with chains of command, and so forth, did not insure predictable and reasonable actions. Rather, I am more interested in three questions regarding viewpoints on MOVE. Was MOVE by nature or by dint of circumstance violent or not? Was MOVE essentially a nurturant or an offensive organization? Was MOVE coherent or incoherent? As I trace a chronology of the group, from the early 1970s to the 1985 confrontation, these three issues are at the forefront. What was MOVE?

MOVE in Powelton Village

John Africa/Vincent Leaphart founded MOVE in the early 1970s. "Who was John Africa?" asks the title of the *Philadelphia Inquirer's* January 1986 magazine article. "He was a quiet, scrawny schoolboy whose teachers considered him retarded. Later he was an interior decorator and a 'smooth dresser.' And then, slowly, he became the messiah of MOVE . . . an incendiary cult that twice stymied the government of the nation's fifth largest city."[4]

A community activist in Philadelphia's Powelton Village (site of the first MOVE house) characterized the founder in this way.

I mean this guy John Africa/Vincent Leaphart was sort of a figure around Powelton well before the MOVE organization. He used to sell horse meat for dogs . . . He sort of seemed like a harmless eccentric, but he wasn't taken very seriously. And then he and this guy Glassey got together and began to develop the MOVE outlook and organization . . . The first thing I remember about MOVE . . . was at this block party that was held by the Venceremos Brigade which sent people to work in Cuba as a fundraiser and MOVE came, this group came in a truck with loudspeakers and basically disrupted the block party . . . They did a heavy rap . . . real revolutionaries are in touch with themselves and are dealing with their lives, and they went into their whole rap about diet and lifestyle . . . there was certainly some consciousness on their part that they were predominantly black and that they were poor. MOVE's philosophy was a mixture of this kind of utopian, romantic back-to-nature stuff and some populist, black nationalist politics . . . Delbert Africa used to be in the Panthers, so there were some ties there . . . the fact that there was neighborhood opposition to them posed a contradiction to them that they tried to resolve by passing it off as like these were people who were instruments of the city.[5]

Sharon Sims Cox, niece of John Africa, represented MOVE and her uncle in the following way in a *Philadelphia Magazine* story:

He was also called the Coordinator then, and he chose the name Africa for us because it showed black identification with Africa . . . People saw John Africa as a harmless man, but he was the one who strategized everything in MOVE. He definitely hated the whole system. He wanted to get rid of everything. He wanted to tear up the blacktop and let food grow everywhere. He wanted to take animals out of zoos and put them back in their environment. He wanted parents to stop beating on their children. He wanted to get back to a time when people were equal and nobody had any more than anyone else . . . MOVE wasn't filthy like people said. There wasn't feces all over. When the kids who didn't have diapers on went to the bathroom, mostly it was outside and we'd dig a hole and cover it like cats do . . . We were the cleanest people in Powelton Village. We constantly cleaned because we had so many dogs and children. We washed windows; we mopped and scrubbed floors every day. We just didn't use soap or deodorant because it's full of chemicals . . . But even those people with strong body odor stopped smelling bad when their bodies got purified from the diet.[6]

Throughout the midseventies, MOVE members continued to demonstrate at various sites and events around the city, and in these demonstrations they continually clashed with the police. "According to one account . . . in a 7-month period in 1975, MOVE members had been arrested on misdemeanor charges more than 150 times, fined $15,000, and sentenced to several years in jail."[7] Of MOVE's various appearances in court and the resulting contempt citations, former MOVE member and sister of John Africa, Laverne Sims, claimed that "because the judge had went to Harvard and Yale and Cornell to learn what the law was, to learn what truth was and then we MOVE come along with what you consider nappy hair and dirty clothes and their style in particular this was like turned them off. They could not understand how a people could stand their [sic] looking as they did and this called for many contempts, many beatings in the courtroom."[8]

Even with these arrests taking place, however, Officer Cresci of the Civil Affairs Unit, a police unit formed in the sixties to "monitor and handle all types of demonstrations and racial incidents," claimed that during the period from 1973 to early 1976 MOVE members, "other than being vocal," were not even *potentially* violent.[9] Bennie Swans, head of the Philadelphia Crisis Intervention Network, made a similar assessment. He responded in the negative to a question by the MOVE commission counsel about potential MOVE violence in the early seventies and went on to add that MOVE was "somewhat strange in the sense of being back to nature and political and progressive but nevertheless very political, very progressive and pretty much concerned about the issues that impacted on the black community."[10]

Yet there was that MOVE language, to which Cresci obliquely referred in the phrase "being vocal." Because MOVE's language has played such a major role in the story of MOVE's presence in Philadelphia and in its representation by authorities, I will be especially attentive to this issue. In a recent publication, *Twenty Years on the MOVE*, MOVE members refer to their expletive-laden language as part of a conscious political strategy: "In demonstrations at zoos, pet shops, political rallies, public forums and media offices, MOVE used non-violent protest and strategized profanity to expose the profane circumstances of the system's injustices" (p. 6). The neighbors in Powelton Village, a neighborhood that was unusually diverse in terms of both race and class and that liked to view itself as tolerant, began to complain about the metamorphosing MOVE house. Neighbors complained of unsanitary conditions, of babies playing in the yard with no diapers on, of rats. In March 1976 a twenty-four–hour police surveillance was set up. In May 1977 several MOVE members appeared on the porch of that house, dressed in jumpsuits and berets and holding rifles. Of the rifles, Janine Phillips Africa stated, several years later when appearing as a witness in the 1985 trial of Ramona Africa, that "I and all MOVE people call these [guns] deterrents because they were inoperable, and the only reason why we had these that could be seen was the police believe in guns, okay?"[11] Symbols slice both ways, however, and Police Commissioner Sambor, asked at the MOVE hearings to give "proof" of MOVE's terrorist status, referred to the symbols of that day as evidence: "pictures of the MOVE organization in 77–78 in uniforms and berets, with automatic weapons in an attack posture on the walls of Powelton Village."[12] MOVE released a statement on the day of the guns, or deterrents, on the porch: "Don't attempt to enter MOVE headquarters or harm MOVE people unless you want an international incident. We are prepared to hit reservoirs, empty hotels and apartment houses, close factories and tie up traffic in major cities of Europe . . . We are not a bunch of frustrated, middle-class college students, irrational radicals or confused terrorists. We are a deeply religious organization totally committed to the principle of our belief as taught to us by our founder, John Africa. We are not looking for trouble. We are just looking to be left alone."[13]

The investigators of MOVE posited a late-seventies transformation of the organization. Questioned by the commission, Bennie Swans referred to that day in 1977: "In my view it seemed to suggest a turning point. Obviously that one day did not reflect just an immediate change, but I guess it was the point [at] which it became clear that MOVE in fact could become a violent organization, would in fact fight, would in fact use weapons in order to accomplish their mission."[14] Police officer George Draper marked a change in his communication with the group: "In the early seventies you could talk to a number of MOVE people. Over the period of time, especially after '78, they became very militant and would not discuss anything with you."[15]

Former MOVE member Louise James defined the change as one of mood: "MOVE principle has never changed. MOVE's mood—and I'm talking about bitterness now—did change." She attributed this change primarily to beatings by police of MOVE members.

> We took the beatings. We took the jailings from 1972 to 1978, prior to 1978, 1977. And in 1977 because MOVE people had been beat so many times—I'm talking about women who were arrested, taken to 8th and Race along with their children . . . But at this period in the history of MOVE neither men nor women ever fought back. They took these

beatings. I'm not just talking about someone walking up to you and pushing or shoving you. I'm talking about the night stick beatings on the head. I'm talking about men who were kicked in the groin repeatedly. I'm talking about hair that was pulled out from the very roots of men and women's heads. I'm talking about one of the brothers whose eyes were nearly pulled from the socket.[16]

Donald Glassey, a graduate of the University of Pennsylvania's School of Social Work in the early seventies, had transcribed John Africa's *Guidelines* and worked with him in MOVE. In 1977 Glassey became an informant for the U.S. Treasury Department's Bureau of Alcohol, Tobacco, and Firearms. He was facing a prison term for falsifying federal firearms forms. The *Philadelphia Inquirer* story on John Africa refers to Glassey's telling a Treasury agent that MOVE had "as the group had warned in its May 20 letter . . . stockpiled bombs. Over the past year, he said, he and other MOVE members had flown to cities across the nation—and London—where they'd left bomb-timing devices, but no explosives, in hotel rooms. These were accompanied by threatening letters warning that MOVE would strike for real if Philadelphia did not stop its harassment."[17]

The final shootout and bulldozing of the MOVE house in Powelton Village in August 1978 followed a five-month-long police blockade of the area around the MOVE house and a failed negotiation process.

MOVE negotiated this agreement with the city, right, to end the blockade . . . The agreement called for them [MOVE] to move within 90 days. They didn't move . . . there were efforts made on the part of different intermediaries to try to find them other places . . . the city's original thing was not only did they have to get out of the neighborhood, but they couldn't reside in a 2-mile radius of the compound, and the city negotiated a settlement that there were no strictures . . . they just had to get out of where they were. The Quakers, there were all these efforts to try to find them a farm . . . and the 90 days came and went and they just didn't leave the compound.[18]

It is interesting to note that, of the seven very active neighborhood organizations that emerged at the time of the blockade, six were either pro-MOVE or willing to engage in negotiation with its members that would allow MOVE to remain (with a perhaps modified house) in the neighborhood.[19]

Nine MOVE members were sentenced to prison terms of thirty to one hundred years for the killing of Officer James Ramp, a policeman shot during the final day of the blockade. The convictions of these nine incarcerated MOVE members became the focus of the remaining MOVE members in the 1980s.

MOVE on Osage Avenue

Soon after I became Managing Director [Goode was managing director of Philadelphia from 1980 to 1982], I started to receive calls from Gerald Ford Africa, from Louise James Africa requesting to meet with me to discuss the 1978, August 8th problem, as they called it. [They said,] "Since the Managing Director of the City had our house torn down on Powelton Avenue, we want you to give us a new house" . . . And that further they wanted me to take the necessary steps to have members of the organization who were in jail released from jail . . . [that they] were in jail to cover up for police wrong conduct and therefore as a black man I ought to do my duty and release those persons from jail . . . I indicated that I did not have the authority to release anyone from jail . . . And the meetings as they went on became progressively more hostile when they determined that I would listen but basically, as they said, not respond, not act or not use my position, use my power to right the wrong that had been committed against them . . . No one ever made a threat to me at all, in any way shape or form nor did they in fact become confrontational with me . . . they said they were hostile towards the system and made their point and their philosophy known to me.[20]

In 1982 MOVE adults (there is no evidence that this group included any of those involved in the 1978 confrontation) and their children took up residence at 6221 Osage Avenue, the home of Louise James in West Philadelphia.

According to MOVE, "By 1983, government officials on all levels had proved ineffective and unwilling to take any action against the unjust imprisonment of innocent MOVE members. The media ignored the issue altogether. In Dec. of 1983 MOVE by-passed the news blackout in a direct appeal to the public by using loudspeakers to inform people of the injustice and the City's conspiracy to eliminate them."[21]

According to the MOVE commission report,

I. By the early 1980's MOVE had evolved into an authoritarian, violence-threatening cult . . . MOVE's last campaign for confrontation began in the Fall of 1983, and was predicated on 1) the unconditional demand that all imprisoned MOVE members be released; and 2) that harassment of MOVE by city officials cease. The stridency and extremism of individual MOVE members escalated during the first years of the Goode Administration. II. The residents of 6221 Osage Avenue were armed and dangerous, and used threats, abuse and intimidation to terrify their neighbors and to bring about confrontation with city government . . . This was achieved by: Both verbal and physical assaults upon targeted individuals living in the neighborhood; the periodic broadcast over outdoor loudspeakers of profane harangues against the government and threats of violence against public officials; the public acclaiming by MOVE of the 1978 death of Officer Ramp, and the repeated threat that, if the police come to 6221 Osage Ave., 'we'll put a bullet in your motherfucking heads'; the prominent fortification of an ordinary row house.[22]

This segment from the report dwells on the several oppressive aspects of MOVE's language in some detail. In fact, the language of MOVE was excessive in three ways. First, in statements issued to the press and in speeches over the loudspeaker, the group indicted the entire social system, its politics and politicians included. They critiqued the newly elected black leaders as well as the more established white leaders. Second, they used profane language to do so, emphasizing through repetition words like *motherfucker*. Third, their language was amplified to an intense degree through the outdoor loudspeaker system. These linguistic excesses wore away at the neighbors over a period of years. At a certain point the neighbors themselves became the targets of the harangues: "Loudspeaker harangues were conducted daily for 6 to 8 hours, through the summer and fall of 1984 . . . A favorite tactic was to target a particular neighbor for a day, during which the unfortunate individual would be subjected to personal attacks filled with accusations of homosexuality, child molestation, promiscuity or sexual inadequacy."[23]

From a police transcript of the MOVE loudspeaker, May 12, 1985:

You black mother fuckin cops out there know that these white cops hate your mother fuckin ass. See y'all cops see you ain't always be here _____ cause I can count them, but mother fucker you is black and you is a nigger and that white mother fucker ain't gonna never let you forget that . . . You mother fuckers don't give a fuck about black folks in South Africa cause you don't give a fuck about black folks here in Philadelphia in this mother fuckin country. You mother fuckers marching around the mother fucking embassy getting locked the fuck up talking about you're against Apartheid but you mother fuckers that's all you're gonna do is march.[24]

MOVE itself, along with at least several commentators, claimed that these speech acts were political, that members of the group would consciously move in and out of quiet language and profanity.[25] One of the group of unofficial citizens attempting to negotiate MOVE out of an armed confrontation on May 13, a group I refer to as organic mediators, elaborated on this ability when describing a meeting with another MOVE member (not residing at 6221 Osage Avenue) on May 10, 1985: "I can't quote the entire conversation, but I can say that he was calm, he was well-disciplined, he was courteous, was articulate."[26] In fact, this issue was explicitly addressed in a statement John Africa read at his 1981 criminal-conspiracy trial: "Our posture of self-defense becomes more crystallized, not through profanity, but in the expressions necessary to assure we are being heard and what is seen as obscenities is simply the necessity to speak louder, stronger, necessitated by conditions we are confronted by . . . a posture of greater volume, a position that is more alarming to reach the subject that is profaned."[27] Both the content and the form of the MOVE language are represented as a self-defense strategy. But the neighbors heard it differently.

Lloyd Wilson, an Osage Avenue resident, recalled:

We tried [reconciliation] but the day the MOVE people came to us a year ago on Mother's Day and they knocked on our door and they said: "We want to let the neighbors know what is going on and get the neighbors' view" . . . And they talked and they told us that they wanted the 13 sisters and brothers out of jail, and that we were to go to politicians, and they preached to us that the system was wrong . . . So the neighbors tried to talk to them and asked them "Well why do you have to be on the loudspeaker with the cussing and stuff with our kids and things around?" And then they tried to explain to us that cussing was nothing and that kids go through worse and and—it just was no talking to them.[28]

Beyond the speech acts, the question of material violence also surfaced for the neighbors. Wilson continued his testimony at the MOVE hearings by referring to a specific incident that turned violent: "Me and my wife had a pretty good relationship with them . . . We had the same philosophy of life, where we had to coexist." That relationship changed on Christmas 1983 when the house was barricaded and the loudspeaker harangues began. On August 8, 1984,

He [Frank Africa] said, "You went to the cops and you told them that I wouldn't move the wood." I said, "Frank, the police were standing right there . . . You don't have to go to the cops to tell them I asked you to move the wood again." He got very indignant and very violent and told me I was a traitor and I would not help support their cause. He got really violent. I didn't understand why he got so upset but I found out later that his mother had visited earlier that evening and he had been chased down the block or something and I walked right into that. Q. Did he assault you at all? Did he hit you? A. Yes he did. Q. Did the police [on the corner] come to your aid? A. No . . . I was very upset.[29]

To the apparently straightforward questions of whether MOVE was violent or not, over time different constituencies gave various answers. City representatives prevaricated in the early eighties. Some, particularly Mayor Wilson Goode, publicly represented the group as an unsanitary and loud nuisance. The main charges against it were License and Inspection code violations and unpaid gas bills. Even after a group of Osage Avenue residents played a tape of a MOVE loudspeaker session to the mayor in the summer of 1984, containing explicit threats against the mayor and the president of the United States, Goode heeded the judgment of federal officials that these threats did not constitute federal offenses and remembered that one June 21, 1984, city memo indicated that "most sustainable charges [against MOVE] are misdemeanors."[30]

Since the May 1977 day of the "guns on the porch" in Powelton Village, however, MOVE had established a reputation among city authorities as at least potentially violent. At one early May 1985 meeting the mayor's office, police surveillance information was tendered regarding the possibility that explosives stolen from Chester, Pennsylvania, might have found their way to the MOVE house on Osage Avenue and that MOVE members might have dug tunnels under the houses and planted the explosives there. And there were scattered reports of physical brawls between MOVE members and other Osage Avenue residents. One such incident in 1983 involved, in apposite Philadelphia fashion, a fight over a parking space originally claimed by MOVE members and later taken by another resident of the block. One neighbor, Carrie Foskey, who saw the end of this fight, claimed that it precipitated a neighbor's petition to the city government to do something about MOVE. Asked by the MOVE commission questioner whether she saw the actual incident, Foskey answered: "No. Only thing I saw. It was almost over. And I saw one neighbor with a stick beating at a MOVE person, who had—that had grabbed him. [Mr. Marshall the neighbor] jumped on his back. They [MOVE members] were biting him from the rear."[31]

Even the very MOVE house at 6221 Osage Avenue was viewed and represented as a threat. An overt and self-conscious transformation of the house had been carried out by the MOVE members over the previous year, culminating in the building of what one member, Mo Africa, called a "bunker" on the roof. The house had been fortified with railroad ties, logs, and steel on the inside and the outside. Mo Africa told a reporter from the *Philadelphia Inquirer* that the bunker was being built "in preparation for a confrontation with the police."[32] However, one policeman involved in the police operation on May 13 could not, in his testimony at the hearings, determine whether the house was an offensive or a defensive structure. On the one hand, he noted that, "if you watch any war movies, you know that is a defensive structure." (This response is an interesting example of the typical postmodern strategy of referring to popular culture images as evidence.) Real scenes of war and cinematic scenes of war slide across each other indistinguishably. On the other hand, he added: "That house in its construction, and in its obvious construction was a threat. I've never seen anything like it in my life."[33]

In a discursive strategy that MOVE members and former MOVE members often deployed, Ramona Africa, acting as her own defense counsel during her 1985 criminal trial (the original charges were criminal conspiracy, riot, and simple and aggravated assault), addressed the following to the prosecutor: "And right now, you know, they have that White House fortified. Are you calling the White House [occupants] criminals?"[34]

By the early eighties, the label *terrorist* was congealing around the MOVE group. In 1982 Carlos Africa was convicted of, among other things, making terroristic threats. City councilwoman Joan Specter called MOVE members "terrorists" in early May 1985.[35] During the October 1985 hearings, at least seven witnesses indicated that they believed MOVE members to be terrorists. However, one needs to recall that at the same time (May 10, 1985) Mayor Goode was making public statements such as, "One ought [not] to engage in violent confrontation over a code violation."[36] And a *Philadelphia Inquirer* editorial of May 5 sent out mixed signals when it claimed that "a small group of malcontents and nonconformists cannot be allowed to continue to intimidate and hold an entire neighborhood and in effect the city government hostage" (p. 6F). Malcontents and nonconformists are not usually associated with hostage holding. Clearly the characterizations of MOVE's capacity and desire to do violence were themselves unstable.

Over time, MOVE's responses to the claim that it was a violent, terroristic organization have been of three types. First, they have emphasized the civic and *familial* nature of the group. Second, they have claimed to be a *religion*. These two assertions comprise oblique responses to the charge of violence, in the logical form of "if we are X we could not be Y." Finally, MOVE has dealt with the charge directly, maintaining that its "violence" was self-defense. Let me give you a sense of how the arguments went.

Former MOVE member Louise James testified that "the neighbors—I have read where the neighbors talked about how the MOVE people attacked them . . . But did the neighbors tell you, for example, how MOVE people baked bread for everybody in that neighborhood and how anybody who wanted that bread could have it . . . how when it snowed . . . MOVE members would get out early in the morning and they would shovel those walks . . . those men would get out there unstintingly and they would spend hours."[37] Accusations of violence are obliquely countered here by assertions of civic virtue and responsibility.

Another former MOVE member, Laverne Sims, more directly countered the violence accusation in her statement: "MOVE members are not terrorists nor criminals. They are life feeling people who have a God given right to adhere to and practice their religion, the law of God rather than man."[38]

Religion as an organizational paradigm was also generated from above by John Africa. A Bureau of Alcohol, Tobacco, and Firearms special agent testifying at the 1981 John Africa trial recounted an interview with the MOVE founder: "I asked him if he knew anything about the Christian faiths. He replied in the affirmative. An example was mentioned of the four Evangelists who, through divine inspiration, wrote four of the books of the New Testamount [sic]. An example was also mentioned regarding the Catholic Church, in which the Pope, who speaking on matters of dogma, was considered infallible by believers. Mr. Leaphart stated that his position in MOVE was something like the above examples, but not exactly."[39]

The assertion of self-defense addresses the accusation of violence most bluntly. First, there is the record of MOVE complaints against the city and specifically the police. Beginning in the midseventies, these complaints of police harassment increased in 1983 and 1984, that period during which all known MOVE locations were kept under surveillance by the Philadelphia Police Department. A police officer in the Civil Affairs Unit on familiar terms with MOVE members through years of surveillance was asked during the hearings if he knew what, if any, action was taken with regard to these filed complaints. His answer was, "No, I did not."

According to police records, these complaints seem to have come primarily in the form of letters and phone calls to the offices of mayors Green and Goode, to prison officials (regarding apparent mistreatment of the incarcerated MOVE members), to radio talk show hosts, and to the Civil Affairs Unit of the police. Many of the communications were perceived as threatening, and follow-ups on the part of the recipients seem sporadic and largely of a defensive nature. Prison officials notified prison workers to anticipate problems, for example. To the following MOVE letter to Mayor Green at the end of his tenure, I can find no response in the files.

December 16, 1983

TO: MAYOR WILLIAM GREEN
RE: MOVE ORGANIZATION

From the MOVE organization, we called your office, an explained our position over the obvious continued persecution. We wanna be able to explain to people we came to you first, so that anything that jumps off you can consider yourself notified. We are not concerned with whether you meet with us or not. We are requesting a meeting to justify what the city of Philadelphia has pushed us to. The request for the meeting is simply to put you on the spot, and protect our position. We don't expect nothing from you, but you can expect *we* are not gonna leave it at that. Everybody in Phila. knows they are innocent, our people's innocense justify our position, we've told you what we are gonna do to stop this persecution and you know what you gotta do if you don't want this situation. The Mayor's office is involved in this entire conspiracy against the MOVE organization, *you* occupy that office, and unless our people are released you gaonna leave the Mayor's office like Rizzo did.

The MOVE Organization[40]

The entire MOVE organization matter was persistently designated a police matter.

Self-defense assertions permeated MOVE's language and interpretations. Recall the characterization of the nonfunctioning guns in 1978 as "deterrents." And, in response to a question by the MOVE commission about the language of MOVE, Louise James provides the key, perhaps, to her sense of the source of MOVE violence: "You acted as though MOVE invented profanity. Profanity came from this system just like violence came from this system. MOVE did not invent it."[41]

The degree to which an alleged underground faction of the MOVE group, named M-1, apparently emergent in early 1983, can be viewed as a self-defense unit is not clear. This shadow organization was referred to by several MOVE members in a January 25, 1983, meeting with officials of the Bureau of Alcohol, Tobacco, and Firearms. The police report of the meeting reads:

> The meeting began at 6:10 PM and ended at 9:20 PM with a lot of rhetoric from MOVE members, but essentially the main facts are as follows:
>
> The MOVE members stated that their leader, John Africa aka Vincent Leaphart PP#232036 instructed them to meet with ATF agents and relay some serious information. They state that the MOVE underground known as M-1, which is a part of the MOVE organization but not under too much control of the organization is upset about MOVE members still in jail throughout the state prison system. The MOVE members present at the meeting state they are non-violent, but are giving this information to prevent anything happening from the M-1 underground organization. The MOVE members stated they are still being exploited by the system, their members put in jail and that all MOVE members in jail should be freed. (A complete 3 hour tape of the meeting is available)
>
> After much discussion the main demands of the MOVE group are:
>
> 1. A meeting with Governor Thornburgh, Ronald Marks, Commissioner of Prisons and Deputy Commissioner Erskine Deramus of the Corrections Bureau.
>
> 2. All MOVE prisoners presently in custody be released because they are innocent.
>
> 3. A letter to be delivered by ATF to President R. Reagan with ATF seeing that the letter gets as far as possible up the line to the President.
>
> It was then stated that if the above is not done the M-1 underground will "take actions" for which the MOVE organization cannot be held responsible.[42]

The minutes of this meeting also reveal the degree to which the stated overt goal of the MOVE members on Osage Avenue was the release of those still incarcerated because of the 1978 confrontation. Thus these members claimed all action on Osage Avenue, including loud-speaker diatribes against political officials and other residents of the block, was aimed at getting those convictions reexamined and, ultimately, getting the MOVE members out of jail.

Concurrent with MOVE's self-generated dossier of complaints against the city, the other residents of the 6200 block of Osage Avenue were actively pressing their case against MOVE in petitions, meetings with elected officials, and letters and calls to the police. The construction of the neighbors' identities through these actions is examined directly in chapter 3.

In all of MOVE's strategies of explanation for its violence, the group met with official resistance. The claim that MOVE couldn't be violent because it was a family and a group with civic virtues was rejected by putting forward opposing images of MOVE's bestiality, its unsanitary cohabitation with dogs, cats, and roaches, and raw meat thrown outside for the animals. The claim that it was a religious organization, although recognized by some past and potential mediators (such as Sister Falakah Fatah of the House of Umoja in North Philadelphia), was rejected where it indeed mattered. For example, prison officials refused to recognize MOVE as a religion, and thus the incarcerated MOVE members were denied the special diet of raw fruits and vegetables that the MOVE organization required.

The claim of self-defense was essentially and automatically dismissed by most city officials and police officers. One interesting counterstrategy against the claim was the focus during the hearings on questions directed to the two former MOVE members about beatings of MOVE members by other MOVE members: "Q. Did you discuss with the Mayor, Mrs. James, any physical confrontations, that you had had with anyone within the MOVE organization? A. I did not. Q. You do not recall talking with the Mayor about being beaten? A. I did not . . . Q. Do you recall telling [Delores Thompson, Civil Affairs Division officer] that your son Frank was ordered to attack you that you were beaten until you started to vomit violently that Frank then placed a pillow over your face and asked John Africa if he wanted you to be cycled. That John Africa [re]plied not at this time?"[43]

Such *internal* violence could hardly be portrayed as self-defense, yet Louise James responded with the related argument that MOVE was, if such accusations were true, certainly not unique in being violent: "If it is relevant that my son beat me or whether or not he did beat me, then I would say it is just as relevant for you to ask Wilson Goode when he comes in here did he beat his wife. I don't think you are going to ask him that."[44]

At the end of the day's testimony Laverne Sims broke through the call-to-recess wrap-up by saying, "Before you recess I just want to make it clear in my mind so I understand, Mr. Lytton [MOVE commission counsel, chief questioner] am I to assume that the bomb was dropped on the MOVE people because Frank beat his mother?"[45]

This question resonated, though it was never again referred to, throughout the hearings. It resonated in the commission's struggle to explore the police plan, first developed in 1984 and then revised for May 13, 1985, to arrest four MOVE members living in 6221 Osage Avenue and to evict at least temporarily all remaining residents. It resonated in the commission's attempt to analyze the precise armaments brought to the scene and used—in the difference, for example, between using Tovex (a civilian explosive) and C-4 (a military explosive). It also resonated in the commission's attempt to determine who was considered innocent (MOVE children? MOVE women? neighbors?) and who guilty (MOVE men? MOVE women? MOVE children?) by the police. And if guilty, then guilty of what?

Unremittingly the commission circled around the "What is MOVE" question, only to have several conflicting images of MOVE proposed. For the commissioners and, I contend, for the city officials who over the years had taken on for themselves the task of dealing (or avoiding dealing) with MOVE, the lack of coherence of the MOVE organization became an issue of contention in itself. I hope to demonstrate with the tools of discourse analysis that there was some relationship between the bomb and the "metaphysical fury," as Bourdieu calls it, at the incoherence of MOVE.

MOVE was called many things in the media and by politicians: "terrorists," "malcontents," "nonconformists," "self-styled revolutionary group," "back-to-nature cult," and "radical group [that] brought primitive lifestyles into the core of modern civilization." Others, at least initially inclined to define MOVE in its own words, used terms like "religious," "progressive," and "political" to describe it. Peter Stallybrass, reflecting on the term *lumpenproletariat*, writes: "The subordinated are, indeed, always vulnerable to representation: [the lower classes] may at most times be represented without restraint."[46] MOVE may have worked, in some senses, to make itself subordinated, to push against all the expectations of moderns social life. However, being a predominantly African-American antisystem organization in America was subordination enough itself. And indeed, we find a "hysteria of naming." On the other hand, the neighbors of MOVE, all African-American, were in *their* subordination under- and unrepresented, the flip side of the proliferation of terms being representational neglect. These neighbors worked hard to be named as normal, rights-bearing citizens, a discursive strategy that ultimately failed in its material effectiveness.

By early May 1985 Mayor Goode was prepared, despite or because of the cacophony of voices about what MOVE was and what MOVE was doing, to follow a very particular line of action. As the MOVE commission final report states: "May 3—The Mayor concludes that an armed conflict between MOVE and the other residents of Osage Avenue is a probability. He asks the District Attorney to reexamine the legal justification for the city taking action against the people residing in 6221 Osage Ave. May 5—Police and prosecutors interview 19 residents [of the 6200 block of Osage] to support applications for search and arrest warrants." (p. 11).

At 5:00 A.M. on May 13, Police Commissioner Sambor was to have read the following statement to the MOVE house via a bullhorn, as he stood positioned at the end of the street: "This is the Police Commissioner. We have warrants for the arrest of Frank James Africa, Ramona Johnson Africa, Theresa Brooks Africa and Conrad Hampton Africa for various violations of the criminal statutes of Pennsylvania. We do not wish to harm anyone. All occupants have 15 minutes to peaceably evacuate the premises and surrender. This is your only notice. The 15 minutes start now."

On the morning of the confrontation, Sambor actually began his statement with the following prologue: "Attention MOVE, this is America. You have to abide by the laws of the United States."[47] The difference between the official and the delivered announcements is telling. In the official version, the MOVE members are simply criminals, about to be arrested. In the delivered version, they are both cultural deviants, defying the culture of America, and criminals, breaking the laws of the state. The police commissioner spoke a certain truth in his delivered announcement. The charges against MOVE and the operation carried out against the group had as much to do with cultural norms of behavior, language, food, and hygiene as they did with the breaking of specific, codified laws.

"Q. Commissioner Sambor, what type of group would you characterize MOVE to be? A. In a word, a terrorist organization."[48]

CHAPTER THREE

The Language of Domesticity

At the beginning of the 19th century . . . norm can no longer stand simply as another name for rule, rather, it comes to designate . . . perhaps most significantly of all, a principle of valorization . . . Its essential reference is no longer to the square but to the average; the norm now refers to the play of oppositions between the normal and the abnormal or pathological.

François Ewald, "Norms, Discipline, and the Law"

Happy families are all alike; every unhappy family is unhappy in its own way.

Leo Tolstoy, *Anna Karenina*

I don't intend to be facetious in quoting Tolstoy on happy and sad families as I begin this chapter. You might reasonably ask, With so much loss of life, displacement, and destruction, how can the "mere" narrative plot of the difference between happy and sad families be offered as a crystallization of the MOVE confrontation? But it is the burden of this chapter to demonstrate that the conflict among the city, the neighbors, and MOVE was portrayed by many of the participants (regardless of their relative power, status, or voice) as precisely that, the story of the relations between many happy families and one sad family. This portrayal drew together, topsy-turvy, as in the cyclone of *The Wizard of Oz,* the paraphernalia of our contemporary culture: Mother's Day, barbecues, dogs and cats, winter coats, hamburgers, and raw sweet potatoes. The objects and habits of people in families and neighborhoods infused the discourse of domesticity, a discourse that played a significant role in construing the conflict. And all of these conjured, before May 13, in the (futile) hopes of preservation, and all deployed, after May 13, in the aim of justification.

The large claim here is that a highly sentimentalized image of family and community pervaded the discourse of the parties to the ultimate conflict. It did so in diverse ways and contexts: in neighbor self-depictions, in meetings with the mayor and other city officials all occurring on holidays, in MOVE counterdepictions, in much police rhetoric of "aftermath," and in media reports. I would like to examine the presuppositions of this discourse and discover the political and strategic roles it played in the conflict among the parties.

First I'll talk about the notions of sentimentality, melodrama, and domesticity (concepts that fit logically together). Then I'll ask a series of questions by way of exhuming the sentimental languages that talked their way through the conflict, the confrontation, and the historicizing aftermath.

Sentimental in *Webster's Ideal Dictionary* (a good, old-fashioned dictionary for these words) has two primary definitions: "1. Of the nature of, or characterized or dominated by, sentiment; as sentimental reasons. 2. Affectedly tender, mawkishly emotion." *Sentimentality* follows: "The quality or condition of being sentimental, especially to excess."[1] Both of these words, then, conjure up normative readings. To accuse—and accuse it seems to be—someone of being sentimental is to suggest that he or she has gone emotionally overboard, that the reaction is mawkish and thus most likely unrealistic or insincere. The words bring to mind a whole series of novels and tracts of the nineteenth century in which angelic children perish while preserving the light of humanity.

Similarly, melodrama entails excess and extremes. Polarized notions of good and evil engage an audience that is permitted no ambivalent reactions.[2] Often, sentimental novels or melodramatic theatrical productions pit a domestic scene, an impoverished but upright home, against an external villain. Thus does domesticity, the images of family, hearth, and home, reside at the heart of sentimentality.

Until the late 1970s literary critics were, by and large, dismissive of sentimental literature (if they read it at all.) They viewed it as a limited, unsubtle, conservative, women's genre. Recently, however, a series of studies has emerged that makes a broader claim for such forms as sentimental fiction, children's penny monthlies, and melodrama.[3] These studies claim that such genres open themselves up to emotion, often going beyond words to essences. Some even reposition the genres ideologically, saying, for example, that the emphasis on generic homes, children, and redemption constitutes a subversive statement against such things as an encroaching, class-stratified market economy and racism by appealing to the "domestic" rights of all people. These studies make readers of sentimental literature aware of its strengths as well as its weaknesses.

And the weaknesses are several. In sentimental visions of social life, traditional figures of domesticity rise to the fore. Images of family crystallize and lock into place. Resulting panegyrics to the intimate, excessive praise of "the little things" that bind our society, often ironically invert the process of expressing and delivering care and diminish the object of concern, precisely through the excess. The outermost symptom of this, absolutely salient in the MOVE case, is rhetorical concern coupled with material neglect. Further, melodrama can flatten the picture of social life, pitting the good against the bad rather than looking for possible points of interaction between parties. As well, sentimental visions, rather than always providing the utopian vistas suggested by the recent theoretical studies, may rely on the assumption of clear-cut, inviolable boundaries between the public and private spheres and lead to exclusionary policies and practices. Writing in the context of a discussion of constitutionalism, Jennifer Nedelsky notes that "the boundary metaphor permits us to indulge in focusing on the experiences we can have in, on, and with our property (whose value I do not deny) and ignore the patterns of relationship shaped by the power to exclude. Private property permits us to flaunt power at the same time that we deny its state-created nature."[4]

Finally, sentimentality, melodrama, and domesticity do not highlight the intellects of the protagonists. Characters tend to engage in symbolic gestures; some are even mute. They may often be children, not as yet educated or relying primarily on cognition. Instinct and the body seem to predominate. One reading of this process is to note that such a reduction places human beings close to other animals, objects at once of sympathy and cruelty, lacking in powers of cerebration. Quoting from one late-nineteenth-century Children's Aid Society annual report (this charitable institution placed putative urban orphans in midwestern farm family settings and produced reports replete with sentimental discourse), Bruce Bellingham notes that, "after conducting their affairs all day the poor do not retire, they 'creep back each night to their filthy lair.' Another Annual Report has a young boy unwrapping a bone 'which he gnawed like a dog.'"[5] Purported bestiality does not elicit official respect.

On the other hand, the sentimental discourse does have its strengths, often precisely in those areas I have identified as weaknesses. It all depends on what tilt is given to the representations. As Jane Tompkins has argued, sentimental discourse can be viewed as authoritative if seen as a strategic discourse deployed against that of the market, for example. It can make claims about the rights to privacy, an area of much current and nuanced constitutional debate, the rights to intimacy, and the rights of the politically powerless, for example, children. Hannah Arendt, writing of the modern interplay between the public and the private realms, makes a similar point, though in a very unsentimental key: "The four walls of one's private property offer the only reliable hiding place from the common public world, not only from everything that goes on in it but also from its very publicity, from being seen and heard . . . The only efficient way to guarantee the darkness of what needs to be hidden against the light of publicity is private property, a privately owned place to hide in."[6]

The association between sentimentality, melodrama, domesticity, and the body can also be viewed in a positive light. These "intensely bodily genre[s]," as Karen Sanchez-Eppler calls them, can make corporeal social actors who are often marginalized by languages of abstraction. This can force the public to identify with those previously viewed as other. We will see this to be true in the MOVE case several times, perhaps never more poignantly than when the forensic pathologist testified before the MOVE commission about the bodily remains of those burned in the MOVE house.

The entire documented history of the conflict between MOVE and the city administration of Philadelphia and residents of homes situated near the MOVE house reverberates with sentimental discourse, melodramatic renderings, and domestic idioms. Chairman William Brown III of the MOVE commission, in his foreword to the commission's final report, even refers to the May 13 confrontation as "a modern morality play . . . in its last act . . . a small war, involving hundreds of participants with a history of its own, with its own martyrs and heroes . . . A police satchel bomb loaded with military and commercial explosives was dropped from a helicopter onto an ordinary, middleclass neighborhood, with a resulting firestorm that laid waste to nearly two square blocks of comfortable row homes."[7] This excerpt contains the melodramatic and domestic. The neighborhood is simultaneously raised up and diminished by its being "ordinary" and "comfortable," creating the doubling effect common to this genre.

At the end of the report another MOVE commissioner, Charles Bowser, has a similar vision. In his individually written opinion, which serves with one other opinion as a coda to the report, Bowser discusses the rescue of the one surviving MOVE child, Birdie Africa (now Michael Moses Ward), by a police officer, James Berghaier. Bowser recreates this moment as a tableau vivant, with the main characters frozen in their poses: "Had not Officer James Berghaier demonstrated the compassion and accepted the duty every adult owes to every child, Birdie would have escaped the flames only to drown in a pool of water. It was a profound moment in the tragic drama of May 13 on Osage Avenue. With the fire raging around them, and gun men lurking in the shadows of the back alley scene that framed them, they were thrown together by policies, procedures, positions and ideologies neither of them fully understood."[8]

Indeed, these two characters are portrayed as mute and innocent in the best of the sentimental tradition. They exemplify rather than elaborate. In this chapter I explore the various ways that relevant actors in this case attempted to exemplify their and others' lives in the idioms of sentimentality, melodrama, and domesticity. I am also interested, however, in the ways that such exemplifications could be and were turned on their heads, the ways that domesticity, for example, could be represented as destructive, false, or corrupt. Such discursive inversion, when practiced in real-life social situations, attests to previously theorized occurrences of discourse dependency and discourse contamination. The argument here is that there are no pure discourses. All rely upon other discursive configurations of the world. Richard Brown talks about such interdependency in his discussion of the "grammars of selfhood" of positivism and romanticism. The latter I take to be similar to the discourse I am broadly construing in this chapter. "These two grammars together form a dialectic of mutual transformation. As opposites, the romantic and positivist grammars dialectically interpenetrate, change and engender each other. Each when carried to its extreme becomes the other."[9]

I don't believe one needs to carry discourses to their extremes in order to excavate the other discourses underlying any given predominant discourses. Because all worldviews, after modernism, must be partial, they all suggest the things they are not. The image of a "happy home" suggests the inverse image of domestic violence, or poverty, for example. It is important to keep these issues in mind as we move through the series of questions that hovered constantly over the development of the MOVE conflict. The questions do not refer to these entities of Family, Child, Neighbor, and so forth as generically understood. They aim to discover how these questions were both asked and answered in and pertaining to this one case.

What Is a Family?

Betty Mapp, one of the neighbors of MOVE on Osage Avenue, was asked the following right off the bat on the morning of her commission testimony: "Q. Do you live alone or do you have a family? A. No. I have a husband. I have three kids, which two kids live with me, and I have a girl, the mother of my two grandsons, also that live with me."[10] Mapp enumerated each member of her family for the commission and provided a sense of their relations to each other. There is a notion of an extended rather than nuclear family here, including the mother of her grandsons, but Mapp proceeded in her testimony to refer to quite standard familial activities they engaged in, in spite of the presence of MOVE: "In October we had a birthday party for one of our grand kids, and I fed the [MOVE] kids then . . . It was early Christmas. We were in making Santa Claus with the kids. We heard this loud noise . . . So we went to the door, and with this loudspeaker, this cursing from the MOVE house saying about they wanted the 13 sisters and brothers out of jail."[11]

There are birthday parties and Santa Claus, holidays taking their most salient root in the family context. A *Philadelphia Inquirer* article of May 13, 1985, describes Mother's Day (May 12) on Osage Avenue, a street tense with anticipation of some kind of confrontation: "It was Mother's Day in the Osage Avenue neighborhood near Cobbs Creek Park and on a sunny day people kept up the rituals of family and love and orderliness." The coupling of family with orderliness is, as will be evident, neither accidental nor trivial. And significantly, children figure centrally in the narratives of these Osage Avenue families that were describing themselves and being described for a larger public. Specific attitudes about relations across generations were expressed almost always in sharp contrast to what MOVE relations were like. For example, Cassandra Carter, another neighbor, recounted an episode in which former MOVE member Louise James had apparently been chased down the street a year earlier by her son, a member of MOVE: "And she was chased down there and told not to come back by her son. And to me, being disrespectful to your parents—if you can't get along then get out of the house, not put your parents out of their house."[12]

Many questions were raised about whether neighbor children played with MOVE children, whether they felt intimidated by MOVE children, and whether their families needed to protect them, either by removing them from the family home, as one neighbor did, or by providing them with mental health counseling and a safe haven (other than the home) during the loudspeaker tirades, as Mayor Goode tried to do.

Two other aspects of family life were described in direct juxtaposition to MOVE: cooking and household pets. A resident of a house next door to the MOVE house described the problems she had with bugs that she thought came from the MOVE house (MOVE didn't believe in extermination). The MOVE commission counsel asked her, "How about your oven?" "A. My oven—to cook dinner, which I was just determined I was going to do because that was my way of life—before I could cook on it I had to turn the stove on and let the bugs evacuate it. This was daily before I could use the stove."[13] Lucretia Wilson was asserting her determination to follow the patterns of her life, including cooking for her family each day. In the background of this assertion are two facts about MOVE. (1) Their philosophy prescribed only uncooked food, largely raw fruits and vegetables. (2) They were very generic in their beliefs about animal rights and included insects and rats in their notion of animal. Thus Wilson asserted her cultural prerogatives against bugs and in favor of cooked food. These assertions become noticeable, we stop to see them as assertions, only in this context of an alternative system.

Finally, Cassandra Carter found a place in her testimony to remember the pets she lost in the fire on May 13. She recounted her speedy evacuation the day before, after the police gave the order for all residents of the block to leave: "And I got some clothes. And I fed my dog and cat because they said I would be back in 24 hours. So I put water and cat and dog food in the cellar for the dog and cat . . . Otherwise I would have taken the dog and cat. I mean a lot of people in that block had animals with them for years. And we had to leave those animals there, because they told us we would be back in 24 hours. Q. And you never got them out? A. No."[14] This reminiscence of pets lost also has its MOVE background. The complaints about MOVE included predominantly MOVE's many barking dogs and the stench from the raw meat put out in the backyard for them. Thus MOVE had its pets too, but they were viewed as menacing in nature and excessive in number. As pets they were not "domesticated," and the raw meat they ate contrasted with the cat and dog food Carter put in the cellar for her animals.

Such homely scenes of family life—holidays, birthdays, cooking, and pets—stand in relief as neighbors testify not only about their conflicts with MOVE and their frustrations with an unresponsive city network of agencies but, perhaps most meaningfully, about their attempts to lead "normal" family lives. I am not suggesting that the self-depictions are self-serving in a crass, opportunistic way. These people had lost their homes, their possessions, and their social lives and were still, in October 1985, in a state of trauma. The depictions are self- and other-serving in a different way. They tend toward a dichotomization of the world. "This is how I do things" opposes the ways that MOVE did things. Moments of generosity and tolerance show up in the neighbors' testimonies, particularly toward MOVE children, but often the final assessment strikes this note: "The MOVE children took over the driveway and they would run up and down the driveway on a flatbed cart. And when the regular children of the block went back there, it was a normal children thing."[15]

Thus there is a sense that the neighbors are establishing their credentials in the hearings as good family people. Issues of class and race run through this process, as I will detail. But in a sentimental narrative, the characters must be sorted out in a fairly simple manner as the hearthbound good or the hearth-threatening bad.

But what about MOVE as a family? Did anyone make or sustain such a claim? And, in constituting such a claim, were the images of family proffered the same as or different from those of and about the neighbors? At one level, given that MOVE had positioned itself as utterly anti-system, we might expect MOVE members and former (but still sympathetic) members to revile the quaint and cozy images of the family in its "ordinary row home." And indeed, though they asserted their standing *as* a family, each member adopting the last name of Africa, they seemed at moments to reject the American sentimental ideal of Family. For example, Laverne Sims was asked to give the age of her son, Chuckie, one of the incarcerated MOVE members, during her testimony at the hearings: "I don't want to seem like I'm being disagreeable . . . MOVE does not believe in birthdays, ages and things like that."[16] Thus in sharp contrast with the celebratory attention given to birthdays of family members of MOVE's neighbors, MOVE does not even acknowledge them.

However, if one listens closely to comments about MOVE made by MOVE members, former members, and MOVE sympathizers, an image of family emerges that closely resembles that of the neighbors. If theories of hegemony are useful, we would expect to find the dominant discourse being spoken even by those positioning themselves in opposition. Thus it merely *seems* strange to hear the language of sentimentality being spoken even by those who are or have been active in MOVE.

Mary Clare Leak, mother of Theresa Africa, an adult MOVE member who perished in the fire, remembered her daughter during testimony at

Ramona Africa's trial: "But my daughter . . . would talk about a lot of the good things about being a MOVE member. She was a very loving girl. She became more loving when she joined MOVE . . . She talked a lot of the MOVE philosophy, the way they lived. And she lived clean. She was drug and alcohol free. She was a very honest—upright girl."[17] According to her mother, Theresa's participation in MOVE seems to have brought her to a state of sublime innocence. *Honest* and *upright* are old-fashioned, staunch words that seem to come from another century. Further, even though an adult woman in the eyes of the law, she is affectionately called a girl. These terms of innocence and tradition are counterposed to the afflictions of our age, drugs and alcohol, thus making her innocence seem that much more remarkable. MOVE is held to be responsible for this character development, is held to constitute a good family.

In Birdie Africa's one-on-one videotaped hearings testimony, Chairman William Brown and he flip back and forth between discussions of gasoline cans on the MOVE roof and discussions of what foods Birdie liked among those offered to him by the MOVE adults. It is a strange and jarring conversation, as much for its oscillations in subject matter as for the content. One series of questions begins with a detailed analysis of the food consumed by MOVE and ends with some speculations on familial discipline and love.

> Q. What do you mean when you say you sneaked food? Food you were not supposed to have? A. Because they eat cooked food and when we would sneak it—. Q. The adults would eat cooked food? A. (Witness nods yes.) Q. How about the children, would they cooked food? A. (Witness shakes head no.) Q. Did you like raw food? A. Some of it. Q. Some of it. What did you like particularly? A. Watermelon, mangos and sweet potatoes and onions. Q. And onions. Did you all eat any meat at all? A. Only one time we ate raw chicken . . . Q. So if you got caught eating cooked food, did they call a meeting? A. (Witness nods yes.) Q. What happened at those meetings? A. They would just get on the person who started it . . . They would say it was wrong and holler at him. Q. Would they ever hit children? A. (Witness shakes his head no.) Q. So you didn't get any spanking or anything like that? A. They don't believe in spankings . . . Q. Do you cry when you were hollered at? A. Yes. Q. Did they say they loved you? A. Yes. Q. Did you love them? A. (Witness nods yes.)[18]

Brown, a kind and soft-spoken man, moves his questions about the checkerboard of modern familial life. Birdie's answers are supposed to give a picture of what it was like in the MOVE family. Food, discipline, emotions, expressions of love—all mix together with bunkers and bombs in his testimony. And no detail, however small, is insignificant for the larger oscillating judgment that hovers over all depictions of the group.

There were those, however, who sought to slice through the familial imagery evoked by MOVE member and sympathizers. Joseph McGill, the prosecutor in the Ramona Africa case, attempted to undermine this image in his questioning of Birdie during Ramona's trial. He was asked by the judge to explain his skeptical line of questioning: "Your Honor, the time period that the defendant [Ramona] has questioned this individual, Michael [Birdie] covered a period of years, saying for many many years you have been with MOVE and the different things about going to the park, selling watermelons and talking to people when you do this, making it seem like a nice little family, which it was not."[19]

While opinions varied on the degree to which the various residents of Osage Avenue did and didn't meet the expectations of a "nice little family," almost all involved in representing these households to a larger public clearly relied on that sentimental image as some kind of ideal. And most of the statements in behalf of this rhetorical ideal circled around the innocent figure of the child at the center of the home.

What Is a Child?

The Grand Duchess: . . . Ah, you should have killed me with him, instead of sparing me.

Kaliayev: It was not you I spared, but the children you had with you.

The Grand Duchess: I know . . . I didn't like them much. (Pauses.) They were the Grand Duke's niece and nephew. Weren't they guilty, like their uncle?

Kaliayev: No.

The Grand Duchess: How can you be so sure? My niece is a heartless little girl. When she's told to give something to poor people, she refuses. She won't go near them. Is not she unjust?

Albert Camus, *Les Justes*

When Philippe Ariès put forward his thesis about the seventeenth-century discovery of childhood as a distinct and valued phase of the life course, he noted that this coincided with a new emphasis on the conjugal family as a unit to be valued beyond its mere association with a name and a genealogical line. Thus the family and childhood, at least in the Western culture surveyed by Ariès, have historically gone hand in hand.

Now to say that childhood and family as real entities are discovered or invented in particular historical moments and contexts is, obviously, to denature them. It is, in the social constructivist line of thought, to say that there is nothing natural about the specific feelings and behaviors that are associated with particular social groupings. Beyond stating that family feelings are social in nature, some important recent studies of changing cultural notions of childhood look closely at the historical transformations in sentiment and at the ramifications of the changes.

Viviana Zelizer's book *Pricing the Priceless Child* looks at the period between 1870 and 1930 in America and analyzes the changing cultural conceptions of childhood during this time. She makes a careful distinction between images of working-class children and images of middle-class children (the mid-nineteenth-century working-class child was publicly construed as having economic value, the middle-class child was viewed as requiring protection from such forces as those of the market). But she concludes that by the 1930s child labor laws and compulsory education destroyed this class difference and all children came to symbolize the sentimental and the sacred, the "priceless." One paradoxical aspect of this transformation, Zelizer points out, is that, while children were no longer expected or allowed to be economically productive, money was still an issue of childhood: "This exclusively emotional valuation had a profoundly poignant consequence: The increasing monetization and commercialization of children's lives."[20] One manifestation of such a monetization is the phenomenon—well said by the title of a *Wall Street Journal* article of the late 1980s, "As Kids Gain Power of the Purse, Marketing Takes Aim at Them"—of children as consumers. Thus do children now come into contact with the market, not as producers, but as consumers.

One possible permutation on the imagery of childhood not addressed by Zelizer involves children's proximity to animals. Such contiguities can slice in two directions. On the one hand are lambs and puppies, symbols of innocence, playfulness, and purity. On the other hand are feral creatures, wolves in the forest. Here are symbols of wildness, ferocity, and bestiality. The former bear no malice, the latter are quite capable of attacking. Much of the tortured ratiocination about the MOVE children focuses on their ontological status: Were they hostages or combatants? Would they hurt the neighborhood children, scare them, or merely play with them? This question lay at the heart of the entire MOVE conflict and confrontation.

Neighbor Children

The neighbors of MOVE on Osage Avenue expressed particular concern that their children were being exposed to damage by the language and actions of MOVE. They spoke of this concern in meetings with the mayor and other elected city and state representatives and with MOVE members themselves. As Mayor Goode recollected: "There was a lot of concern on the part of those residents about their children, about the fact that these children had to indeed listen to night after night of profanity, all types of vile language, all types of accusations against them and the neighbors, threats against public officials, and felt that something ought to be done."[21]

Goode's response was to develop a plan to provide mental health counseling for the neighbor children and to remove them from their homes to the Cobbs Creek Park Recreational Center during the times of greatest loudspeaker use. Removal was the only offered form of protection from language that was believed to be contaminating.

Osage Avenue block captain Clifford Bond relates a specific moment of exposure and develops a narrative of morality around it: "When an individual [MOVE member] was on the roof with the mask and the shotgun, my daughter was in our picture window and she said, Daddy what is that man doing on top of the roof with the gun? And I didn't have an answer. She asked, and she was about four or five years old then—she asked, isn't that against the law? And I said yes. Then what I began to observe with this contradiction lies on the street that it begins to affect my children by questioning what's right and what's wrong and I really don't appreciate that."[22]

A home has a picture window in order that those who live there can look out onto a world of pleasant pictures. The concept of *picture window* is not meant to evoke images of men on roofs with guns. The curious and perplexed voice of a child developing a sense of laws is framed here by that window out of which she looks. It is, as Bond notes, a scene in which a "contradiction lies on the street." And the power of this scene, a quiet scene partially insulated from direct confrontation, derives from the image of the innocent child at its center.

Throughout their preoccupation with their own children's well-being, the neighbors of MOVE expressed ambivalence toward the MOVE children and the interaction between the "regular" children and those of MOVE. But the neighbors often adopted a transcendent vision. Betty Mapp answered a question about the children's interactions: "Commissioner Chinn: Mrs. Mapp, did the MOVE children ever play with the neighbors' children? Mrs. Mapp: Yes. Commissioner Washington: They did? Mrs. Mapp: The neighbors' children, my grandchildren. Some of the neighbors said to me, they used to say, 'I see you feeding the kids and stuff.' So I explained to them that kids is kids and you can't go to one child and say don't play with another child, because kids are kids . . . So then all the kids used to come on my side and play with the MOVE kids, the little kids their size, down in the back."[23]

Before I explore the alternating images of the MOVE children that circulated during and after the conflict, I want to look closely at a specific question about the respective statuses of MOVE and neighbor children put to city officials testifying at the MOVE commission hearings. This question, repeated several times, attempts indirectly to gainsay the thinking of these officials at the time of the development of the May 13 plan and on the day of its execution. It is utterly key to my analysis of the deployment (and points of breakdown or discursive contamination) of the language of sentimentality in this case.

"If you had learned that the MOVE people in 6221 Osage Avenue had taken one of the neighbors' children and had that child in the house, would you have done anything different on May 13 than you did?" Mayor Goode, to whom this question is posed in a slightly variant way, answered: "Had they been kidnapped . . . Probably so, yes. I'm not sure. I would have to be given some real facts to deal with a given point of time."[24] The police commissioner replied: "Yes sir, considerably different . . . Q. Could you explain why you regard a neighbor's child differently than, let's say, a seven-year-old child of the MOVE organization? A. Because a neighbor's child is a negotiable entity. It is—and a hostage is one who is there under threat of danger, threat of loss of life, to be able to bargain. MOVE has never bargained . . . MOVE has never threatened to harm their children. They have always dared us to harm them."[25]

Something profound is happening around this question. For one thing, it suggests that MOVE might have been capable of kidnapping, a crime they never committed. On another level, the question might be heard as a sentimentalist setup—we dare you to claim that neighbor children are more valuable, more worthy of saving than MOVE children. And, in fact, neither respondent does say exactly that. Neither denies some difference, however, even though both hypothetical children are the same age and caught, in some way, in the same house. For Goode, the difference is not articulated and seems to rely upon some contingency of "real facts." Somehow, he implies, the situations would *have* to be different. Sambor is more direct, cutting a swath through the sentimental with the tactical. A military discourse names "negotiable entities," "hostage," "bargain," and "threat." Sambor, in essence, denies the sacralizing rhetoric, reinscribing the category of child in the apparently all-encompassing discourse of strategy.

The point is, however one slices it, neighbor children were viewed as different from MOVE children and the repercussions of their perceived ontological difference spread widely through the neighborhood and the city administration to the plan and the operation of May 13.

MOVE Children

On May 7, 1985, at the mayor's office, several city officials met to discuss the possibility of arresting some of the MOVE members at 6221 Osage Avenue. During this meeting the participants read a memo sent from the district attorney's office to the mayor. In the memo the MOVE children are mentioned in the context of their possible status as hostages of MOVE. Managing Director Brooks was questioned about this memo during the hearings in an illuminating segment of his testimony.

> Q. Do you recall any discussion at this meeting on May 7, 1985 concerning this statement that the police believed that MOVE would use their children as hostages?
>
> A. And I do recall [a] discussion which says great care must be used as pertains to the children . . . I might add that the use of the word "hostages," when put in quotations to some degree, and I don't know to what degree, colors the use of word "hostages." Had the word not been put in quotations it might, might have made some difference in what somebody did. But I don't know that that did or didn't.[26]

I would be reckless to blame a bomb or an unfought fire on a pair of quotation marks, but this passage does make the power of discourse evident. The subtle distinction between hostages and "hostages" is not lost on Leo Brooks. It may indeed have influenced the interpretation of the mayor's dictum to those charged with creating the plan that they keep "in mind at all times that there were children in the house. And we did not want to do anything that would harm the children inside the house."[27]

The long history of the relationship between the city and MOVE had embedded within it the relationship between the city and MOVE children. This history encompassed one incident in which MOVE charged that city police had killed a MOVE infant in a fight between police and MOVE members, other incidents of city agency concern with MOVE children's physical conditions (including one official medical check up of some of them), and Managing Director Goode's intervention with the

Pennsylvania Department of Welfare to provide food stamps for MOVE children in the early 1980s. In the final weeks before the May 13 attempted arrests, Mayor Goode had directed the managing director to go through the Department of Human Services and the Law Department to "pick up the [MOVE] children in the park when they left home . . . and then go in and see a judge and ask the judge to permit us to keep them through the date that we would decide on."[28] The police learned of this directive but, for a variety of reasons, never actually picked the children up.

In the meantime the exact ontological status of these children was contested rhetorical terrain. Were they kids, plain and simple, similar in all respects (except appearance and diet) to the other neighborhood kids? Were they feral children, growing up wild in the middle of civilization? Were they guerrillas-in-training, similar to children caught in wars and resistance movements in such places as Afghanistan? Answers varied.

In the Philadelphia community survey carried out by the American Friends Service Committee, "almost everyone explicitly recognized the children as innocent victims." However, at the same time there was considerable reluctance among respondents to characterize the children as hostages. This was not the same reluctance as that expressed by Commissioner Sambor, for example, who framed his categorizing decisions in a strategic manner. Rather, the community members interviewed did not want to assert that MOVE adults were capable of holding their children hostage. Mr. M notes, for example: "I believe they were victimized as . . . the adults were victimized. I despise that hostage word in this situation. I can't separate the children from the adults. It's their own little community."[29]

The neighbors of MOVE on Osage Avenue had a more ambivalent and detailed reading of the MOVE children. Inez Nichols recollected a specific encounter with the MOVE children: "It was in the winter. It was either around Thanksgiving or Christmas and [my husband] said: Look, and the children were huddled together like, I would say, cattle for warmth and they had on something like a sweatshirt or something, you know and it was very cold and they had yellow mucus, some of them did, coming from their noses and he said for me to go buy those babies some coats."[30]

Nichols's depiction of this scene conjures up all the elements of a Dickensian tale. A winter's day, the aura of holidays and familial celebrations, children in the cold, and a gesture of kindness. The children here are portrayed as animals. Not wild, savage animals, rather "cattle," domesticated and dumb. And while their ages varied (in the official estimates) from around five to thirteen, they are called "babies." Babies are indeed the most innocent of humans, if only because they have not yet had a chance to know and act in the world.

In a very different vein Cassandra Carter suggested that the MOVE children were more akin to guerrilla fighters: "At some time they used to have the children on the bull horn to say things just like they were—it was like—the only way I can say is it is like what the men say when they come back from Viet Nam or whatever, that children would walk up to them and the children would have explosives. Those children were almost as dangerous to some people as the adults were because they were being trained in the same tactics as the adults were."[31]

The analogy to Vietnamese children and explosives is significant. The specter of Vietnam, its weapons, personnel, psychological damage, hung heavily over the MOVE conflict and confrontation. The idea that MOVE children were like other children fighters was not confined to some of the Osage Avenue neighbors. Police Commissioner Sambor suggested as much in his response to a statement of MOVE Commissioner Chinn. "Q. Now, we know that the children wasn't doing any shooting. So what about the civil rights of the children? Do you feel that their rights— A. I do not know that the children were not shooting."[32]

For Ramona Africa, the only MOVE adult who survived the May 13 fire, it was the MOVE children's purity itself that drew the wrath of the city. She claimed that the bomb was dropped on purpose to kill the children because they were the only pure MOVE members raised in MOVE, outside the system. I take a closer look at that notion of purity by focusing on the case of the sole surviving MOVE child, Birdie Africa.

The Case of Birdie Africa

Birdie Africa, the son of Rhonda Africa and Andino Ward (not a MOVE member), was a slight thirteen-year-old when he escaped the fire on May 13. His story as recounted by police officers, the media, his father, the MOVE commission, and himself is very much to the point of the questions posed in this chapter. It also takes these questions—for the most part aimed at locating and discerning the sentimentalizing or melodramatizing discourses in this case as well as their discursive detractors—and draws them out further, for the case of Birdie reveals a moment in which a discourse is brought to bear on the reshaping of a life.

BIRDIE'S ESCAPE AND RESCUE. Somehow both Ramona Africa and Birdie Africa were able to escape from the burning house at 6221 Osage. However, they escaped into a back alley filled in the evening of May 13 with water and downed electrical wires.[33] Ramona was able to climb onto a partitioning wall in the back but was unable to pull Birdie up with her. Birdie fell, on his back into the accumulating water and debris. Here the narrative continues in the words of a stake-out police officer positioned in the alley, James Berghaier: "Tommy, here take my shot gun, I said, I'm going to go get the kid. Officer Mellor stated Jim be careful, it could be a trap. And I reiterated, It's only a kid Tom. I remember Birdie just laying there . . . As a result of Birdie falling on the concrete, that was legit." Berghaier did wade in and carried Birdie out of the alley. Berghaier recounted that Birdie was saying to him, "Don't shoot me, don't shoot me. My pants are falling down. I'm hungry. I want something to eat." After handing Birdie over to those who would drive him to the hospital to begin treatment for his burns, Berghaier said to him, "Take care son, it's all over with."[34]

Officer Berghaier was a character in Commissioner Bowser's melodramatic tableau vivant, thrown together with Birdie "by policies, procedures, positions and ideologies neither of them fully understood." As the evidence mounted up, it wasn't clear that anyone involved in this case, including the mayor and the police commissioner, understood or controlled the bureaucratic policies and procedures. In this, Berghaier was not alone. And yet, as the single police officer who *gives away his gun* to approach a MOVE child, he is singled out both for his heroism and for his lack of understanding. Berghaier announces that Birdie is "just a kid" and names his fall as "legit." Thus he refutes his partner Tommy Mellor's assessment that this might be a trap. Mellor is not alone in his suspicion. Another officer, Walter Washington, was almost simultaneously involved in taking Ramona into custody. He had a very different narrative to tell about his experience than that of Berghaier: "I had an experience once when I was in the service, when I was in Vietnam. We tried to apprehend some people surrendering . . . and one of the females was wired and subsequently we all got the wrath of shrapnel. The people who were up in front were killed. And that's the first thing came to my mind. I thought maybe I should check her and see if she were wired."[35]

Here Vietnam once again intrudes into West Philadelphia in the mideighties, bringing its memories and flashbacks and suspicions of apparent innocence with it. But what is key here is that Berghaier articulates his rejection of such a wartime mode of thinking in his phrase "only a kid." The MOVE commissioners cling to this scene in their later references to Berghaier's heroism. His actions are used to center narrative of the event to the degree that they assert the uncomplicated childness of Birdie, no longer "hostage," "combatant," or "animal."

Once at the hospital Birdie was treated for his burns and was fed, of all things, given his diet of raw fruits and vegetables, hamburgers. Thus said the *Philadelphia Inquirer* of May 15, 1985: "And for Birdie Ward Africa, the 13-year-old boy discovered naked after Monday's fire bombing of MOVE's Osage Avenue compound, there were hamburgers" (p. 16A). In this media report Birdie lost his pants but gained a hamburger. It is as if the hospital workers swiftly effected his move from primitivity to civilization.

This mixing and matching of objects of American culture persists as a theme in all stories told about Birdie. It is as if the coupling or uncoupling of Birdie with such objects becomes proof (or not) of his childness and, ultimately, his normalcy.

The further scene of almost humorous pathos—pants falling down, requests for food—just emphasizes this. Only a "kid" could emerge from a daylong siege, ten thousand rounds of fired ammunition, tear gas, explosions, water, and a horrific fire and immediately ask for something to eat.

LIFE AFTER MOVE. By the time Birdie Africa testified in the MOVE commission hearings on October 31, 1985, his name and life had changed substantially. He was living with his father and was called Michael Moses Ward. The lawyer representing him had a rather long opening statement to read (not in Michael's presence) about Michael's life as Birdie Africa. This statement weaves a precise story of innocence deformed and of longing.

> It should be recalled that for almost 90 percent of his life, starting from the point where he was a baby, until May 13, 1985, Michael was in the custody and control of the adult members of the MOVE organization, about whose life style and program, such as it was, you have already heard much . . . to our surprise and disappointment, there have been some casual references to him as a MOVE member . . . Michael Ward was, of course, no more a member than a child of Republican and/or Democratic parents would be styled by a particular party label. He was throughout an absolutely innocent, guiltless, and under the circumstances, vulnerable child and then youngster . . . Experts have concluded that his physical growth and development have been compromised perhaps permanently, most likely due

to protein deficiency in his diet . . . he was not in an environment which conforms with prevailing social, cultural and educational standards. Michael was never permitted to play with toys. He was never permitted to watch television. He was never permitted to attend school.[36]

While it straightforwardly asserts Michael's overall innocence, this statement constructs such innocence out of various bits and pieces of our culture: protein, experts, school, television, political parties, and toys. In some ways it is astonishingly honest about the mélange of cultural artifacts that do tend to all get presented as equivalents in most cultural products. There is no attempt to *evaluate* the relative merits/faults of such things as protein and television, for example. Michael was deprived of them all, and the implication is that all of these things need to be restored to him.

Michael's testimony itself consists of a series of answers Birdie gives (usually one- or two-word answers) to chairman Brown's questions. His testimony as a whole is remarkable in its almost seamless transitions from discussions of MOVE trips to the Italian market in south Philadelphia to buy fruits and vegetables, to its discussions of gasoline cans on the roof, to Michael's capacity to recognize which guns the police were carrying on the day of the confrontation. Brown is most gentle with Michael, who now sports a jacket and has his dreadlocks shorn. And yet, despite Brown's acknowledgment that Michael experienced love in MOVE, the narrative text has a tendency to tease out Michael's yearnings to be a "normal" kid while he was in MOVE and his satisfaction with his ongoing transformation. "Q. And in those days people called you 'Birdie'; is that right? A. Yes. Q. And now your name is Michael? A. Yes. Q. [I] like Michael. It is a good name. How do you like Michael? A. I like it. Q. You like it." "Q. Did you ever think about leaving MOVE? A. Yes . . . A long time ago . . . Because you couldn't do what other kids do. Q. What were the other kids allowed to do who were outside of MOVE that you couldn't do? A. Play with toys and stuff and ride bikes and watch TV."[37]

Thus does Brown draw out the desire. But a few points of slippage in the text problematize the apparent total "otherness" of Birdie's MOVE existence. For example, when Michael is asked how he knew he was hearing a gun being fired on May 13, he says that he had previously heard guns on television. This and other moments suggest that there was more interpenetrating of "normal" and MOVE cultures than is being acknowledged in the unsubtle narrative of before and after.

The "after" for Birdie/Michael is ostentatiously presented in a *Phila-delphia Inquirer Sunday Magazine* article appearing some three years after the fire. The title, "The Miracle of Birdie Africa," is telling. The miracle is the transformation from wild child to normal teenager, and the article provides the details of the transformation. Birdie/Michael's father, Andino Ward, is given total credit for the effected redemption. And indeed, he does seem to have utterly devoted himself to bringing Birdie/Michael back to health, debriding his burn scars in an arduous and frequent process of baths and scrubbing. What is striking to me about the narrative current of the article, however, is the emphasis on the rejection of MOVE behaviors and habits and the utter embracing of American middle-class, consumer culture. This emphasis appears to derive from Andino Ward and is reproduced by the article's author: "Andino brought gifts from the outside world—puzzles, a Walkman, a Rubik's cube. Birdie had been taught that toys and games were evil inventions, but the presents enchanted him. For years he had hungered for the forbidden life of a normal child . . . [Amal] was running the bath water when Birdie asked for a sweet potato. 'I thought, there is no time like the present to start rearranging his thought process.' Andino said: 'I told him, "No, you cannot have a raw sweet potato. That's over. You did that in MOVE . . . You're going to have to eat normal foods like everyone else.'" And finally, transformation complete, "it is Saturday morning, the day after Michael was grounded . . . Even so, Michael is sunny and pleasant as he devours scrambled eggs, pancakes, bacon, milk and juice. He mows the lawn and then gets his hair cut at the local barber shop . . . Andino gives Michael a big hug and teases, 'What kind of haircut is that?' . . . 'I wanted to get it like that kid on *The Cosby Show*,' [Michael] explains."[38]

Here are the toys, the foods, and the television of which Birdie Africa had been deprived. They are the markers, the calibrators of normalcy (a word that is repeated throughout the story). The raw is rejected for the cooked, the Rastafarian model rejected for the Cosby model. Choices are always being made, and it seems American culture comes whole-cloth. There is no sense of irony in the narrative of this transformation; indeed, it seems cruel to begrudge Birdie/Michael these everyday icons of the dominant culture, even here in the pages of an academic study. Yet, given all the other extant discourses of television rotting children's minds and high cholesterol clogging their arteries, the complete absence of a critique of the wholesale acceptance of these behaviors by Andino Ward as cultural transmitter is striking. Is this really what we need to hear of Birdie/Michael to believe that MOVE has been excised from him? May nothing of MOVE be allowed to remain if Birdie/ Michael is indeed to be recognized as a child?

One last question was posed to Michael as he testified before the MOVE commission: "Now Michael do you know what it is to tell the truth about things?" What fascinated me about this question was not, or not simply, the implication that MOVE might have had *no* system of truth and falsity but rather that no other witness at the hearings was asked this question. Somehow, one wonders why it is assumed that adult witnesses know what telling the truth is or that the concept is itself so simple and unproblematic. And how would such a basic epistemological and normative-oriented question indeed be answered?

What Is a Neighbor and a Neighborhood?

While there have been many ethnographic studies of neighborhoods and communities, few seek to analyze precisely what it means to be a good neighbor. Parents of small children reading this may involuntarily flash on Mr. Rogers with his sublime and cheerful division of labor among the residents and his neat and tidy studio-home: sweater in the closet, curtains on the windows. Indeed, that is a rather benign, if excessively conforming, image. It does, however, participate in the sentimentalizing discourse of what a neighborhood ought to look like. It is just such an image that was superimposed on the necessarily more complicated reality of Osage Avenue.

There have been studies of neighborhood communities in sociology and anthropology. From *Small Town in Mass Society* by Vidich and Bensman to *Canarsie* by Jon Reider, these studies have examined issues of class, race, and power. Reider's study focuses on the issue of maintenance of group boundaries in the face of demographic change. And of course, boundaries are important in the MOVE case. But they are important in a more subtle manner. In this predominantly African-American community, the emergent boundaries had less to do (at least before the actual police operation commenced) with race and more to do with class and life-styles. Randall Collins writes that "it is the group boundaries that determine the extent of human sympathy; within those boundaries humanity prevails; outside them, torture is inflicted without a qualm."[39]

The group boundaries on Osage Avenue were rather fluid for a significant period of time, with MOVE being more or less included in the active notion of "neighbors." This seems to have been true both for the other residents of the block as they saw MOVE and for MOVE members as they saw the other residents. Only in 1984 did the boundaries begin to harden and the "us versus them" reading take over.

Before looking in detail at the circulating images of neighbor, home, and neighborhood, I would like to introduce the concept of the "reasonable resident." Anthropologist Boaventura de Sousa Santos develops his idea of the topos of the reasonable resident in his study of a squatter settlement in Rio de Janeiro. He builds up his notion from an analysis of a series of cases of conflict among the residents in the town he calls Pasargarda. In his discussion of case 11 the reasonable resident notion is most salient. This case has some strong resemblances to the MOVE case.

> When repairing his house Mr. KS extended one of the walls so much that the street, already very narrow, was almost completely obstructed. Some neighbors complained before the Resident's Association. The presidente and one director inspected the locale and concluded that the street had been virtually closed by the construction. They went to see Mr. KS and explained the situation to him. He was reluctant to do anything about it but the officials pushed the matter vary hard. The argument was: "Look, if someone dies, the coffin cannot pass down the street. Not even the street cleaner's wheelbarrow." Faced with the refusal of Mr. KS to cooperate, the presidente said: "Look, I think that's unreasonable. But in any event you know that the Association has powers to demolish unlawful buildings in Pasargarda. I have the laws here and I can show them to you. And the police are anxious to help the Association enforce its powers." The presidente and the director left without Mr. KS making any commitment. Shortly after the discussion Mr. KS decided to demolish the wall himself and to rebuild it according to its original dimensions.[40]

Like Mr. KS, MOVE members also built a wall, across the back alley, that effectively cut off access to several of their neighbors' driveways. And like the Pasargarda neighbors, the neighbors of MOVE objected to this construction, both to MOVE members and to elected officials, on grounds of reasonableness and safety. If we extend the comparison to include the MOVE neighbors' complaints about the overall effect of MOVE members' piling up wood within and over the boundary of their own backyard and their provision of raw meat (left out in this yard) to their animals, and so forth, we can include neighbor complaints about health and hygiene issues. It is illuminating to go back to the two examples employed by the presidente to demonstrate the unreasonability to

Mr. KS—those of the coffin and the street cleaner's wheelbarrow. Of these images de Sousa Santos writes: "[Mr. KS's] conflict is not only with those who live on his street but also with those who die in Pasargarda and whose coffins have to pass through the street on the way to the cemetery. Mr. KS is violating the interests of the living and the dead . . . His transgression extends beyond the neighborhood in another sense: it damages the community interest in cleanliness because it prevents the street cleaner . . . from carrying the rubbish in his wheelbarrow to the entrance of Pasargarda."[41]

The topos of reasonability is being construed here as acting in the collective interest in such identified terms as hygiene, generational relations, and public access. Compare this with an excerpt from a March 8, 1985, letter from a group of MOVE neighbors calling themselves the "United Residents of the Sixty-two Hundred Block of Osage Avenue" to the governor of Pennsylvania, Thornburgh: "Move has blocked off our driveway and denies us full access to it. They stand, in (the house they stole) violation of every health and safety ordinance enacted since the plague. All winter long they have scavenged wood which they burn inside the house and on the roof!!"[42] The neighbors also complain of the loudspeaker noise and profanity and of the threats MOVE members had made against them. Clearly, there are distinct parameters of good neighborliness that, like those in Pasargarda, are being appealed to in this case against MOVE, hygiene and safety issues codified in laws heading the lists.

The Neighborhood of Osage Avenue

According to the 1985 annual report of the Urban League of Philadelphia, by 1980, 162,448 out of a total of 638,878 black residents of Philadelphia lived in West Philadelphia. Of these residents, 51.9% owned their homes. Osage Avenue, a block on the border of West Philadelphia and the Philadelphia suburbs, was a predominantly homeowning block. The Urban League calculated that approximately 25% of the annual income of black homeowners went toward costs of ownership during the period of the early eighties. Thus it was with considerable commitment that black people brought and maintained their homes in West Philadelphia neighborhoods.

In her book about the relocation efforts of the city after the destruction of so many of these homes in 1985, LaVon Wright Bracy, Mayor Goode's administrator in charge of that effort, charts the racial demographic history of the neighborhood. In doing so, she also charts its continuity.

There were eight black families that moved to Osage Avenue in the late fifties; seven of them still resided there as of May 13, 1985. Of the original nine black families that moved to Pine Street during this same period, eight of them still remained as of May 13 . . . By 1962, the ratio was seventy percent black and thirty percent white living on Osage Avenue. At the same time, the south side of Pine Street was forty-one percent black and fifty-nine percent white. By 1965, the south side of Pine was sixty percent black. By the early seventies, the block was completely black, while on Osage Avenue, blacks comprised ninety percent . . . Osage Avenue and the south side of Pine Street could be best described as a stable community with mature residents who loved their environment and took pride in their surroundings. More than half of the residents living in the sixty-one homes which were destroyed had been there for more than twenty years; more than half were married; over twenty percent were widowed, and ten percent retired.[43]

Osage Avenue intersects a larger, winding road across from the rolling and leafy Cobbs Creek Park. It was a narrow street of row houses. William Brown referred to the street as being composed "of comfortable row homes" and being an "ordinary, middleclass" neighborhood. Bracy noted stability, maturity, love of environment, and "pride in their surroundings." Class issues were actually not all that clear, as I'll show below. But for the moment if we read "ordinary" as "normal" and recall the at least discursive deference paid to the normal and the reasonable, we can begin to understand Brown's, Bracy's, and others' choice of terms at a deeper level.

The mass media consistently stressed the pride, stability, and orderliness of the block of Osage Avenue that was disrupted by MOVE. Some phrases in the *Philadelphia Inquirer* were "this block is one of row houses where people live more closely together and where the rules of good neighborliness are of utmost importance" (May 10, 1985, p. 16A); "the house-proud, middle-class, stable community" (May 13, 85, p. 6A); "what should the response of government be when a violence-prone, self-styled back-to-nature cult moves into a house in a traditional working-class West Philadelphia neighborhood and disrupts the peace, tranquility and quality of its neighbors' lives?" (May 5, 1985, p. 6F). Charles Bowser, in his book on the MOVE confrontation, wrote of his visit to one neighbor's home: "It was a neat, modestly furnished home which, like so many other Philadelphia row houses, seemed to welcome visitors with a warm embrace."[44]

On the surface, these representations of Osage Avenue appear to be highly and unproblematically laudatory. This is a *good* neighborhood. But something seems oppressive in the precise words chosen, a feeling of normative and physical claustrophobia. Is it pushing things too far to claim an implicit sense here that row houses require more tidiness, more tranquility, more conformity than tract homes or mansions? In other words, that rich people have more, and are *acknowledged* to have more, social freedoms to be loud, untidy, eccentric? At any rate, the repeated stress on such diminutive terms as *comfortable* and *orderliness* reflects something about the dominant culture's unconscious condescension toward the cultures of minorities and those not in the upper classes.

These kinds of descriptions always make me suspicious because they are so pat and so uncomplicated, so without the dynamic tension of life—even more so when those being so defined participate in such descriptions themselves: "Your Honor, we are a small working class block of 39 row houses. We take pride in our homes, and we once cherished the underglow of peace we felt just living here."[45] Now it is very likely that the residents of Osage Avenue did like living on their block and, before the arrival of MOVE, did feel that they had constructed a good neighborhood. It is also very likely that the identified social structural problems of our larger society had some effect on the lives of those on Osage. I cannot say what these were with any certainty. There are only hints, here and there. It is also not my aim to vilify the neighbors of MOVE. However, it is my aim to problematize a sentimental discourse, to demonstrate its insufficiencies and its ramifications.

One example comes from Bowser's book, which is generally laudatory toward the neighbors. He provides a hint of a pre-MOVE life more complicated than the dominant image suggests: "Prior to their problems with the MOVE house, the only serious neighborhood tension was engendered by fights between black teenagers from their neighborhood and their white counterparts from the suburban towns. They had intermittent territorial clashes in the [Cobbs Creek] park."[46]

Located on the border between predominantly black West Philadelphia and predominantly white Lansdowne, Yeadon, and other Philadelphia lower-middle-class suburbs, the 6200 block of Osage Avenue was on a frontier. Neighborhood territory has always been an issue for teenagers in Philadelphia (which in the 1960s and 1970s had a severe gang problem). Racial composition of neighborhoods has been and continues to be an issue. Bowser's brief and casual news bulletin from the pre-MOVE past makes intuitive sense.

The former MOVE members testifying at the hearings also suggested in a more direct and overt way, that the neighbors of MOVE may have engaged in some of the same practices for which MOVE was criticized. Laverne Sims stated: "Do you think for one minute there is not a neighbor on Osage Avenue who does not use profanity? It is unreal, isn't it to believe that all out of a block of people the only one used profanity was MOVE."[47] Sims made a similar comment regarding the neighbors' capacity to be violent (a capacity the neighbors themselves acknowledged when in the spring of 1985 they publicly threatened to "take matters into their own hands"). Along these lines are neighbors who testified to having had guns in their homes. After one fight between a MOVE member and the son of one neighbor, Nathan Foskey, Foskey called the police and then took his own preventive action: "We had a gun in the house. I took the gun and I took the bullets out in the basement and hid them and put the gun in the second floor drawer, bedroom drawer to make sure I had thinking time in case another such incident occurred and I might not be in control."[48]

This image of a neighbor with a gun collides with the images of an "underglow of peace." Perhaps this and other acknowledged guns were all purchased as a response to the threat of MOVE. Perhaps the neighbors always had guns. In one sense, it doesn't matter. What matters is that, if one reads and listens closely enough, a more three-dimensional picture of Osage Avenue emerges than that presented by the dominant sentimental discourse.

It is also true that there was a critical difference between MOVE's use of profanity and demonstration of weapons and neighbors' alleged uses of profanity and ownership of guns. This difference revolves around the issue of public and private domains. Recalling Hannah Arendt and "the darkness of what needs to be hidden against the light of publicity," our culture differentiates between what is legitimate public behavior and what should and can occur only in the privacy of our homes. While it is true that the constitutionally recognized right to privacy is a constant source of judicial debate and legislative initiatives, it is also true that there is a predominant cultural recognition of that right and of the concomitant need to constraint certain behaviors in the public domain. So if the neighbors of MOVE cursed, handled a gun, or slandered their neighbors in the privacy of their own homes, that behavior would not, despite the former MOVE members' assertions, function in the same manner as MOVE members cursing over the loudspeaker, MOVE members on the roof with a gun, or the loudspeaker "character assassinations" of the neighbors. One might read this assertion of difference as being hypocritical, and there are moments of enacted squeamishness by testifying police officers at the hearings, by MOVE commissioners asking questions, by the *Philadelphia Inquirer*, among others, when it seems that no "decent" person has ever said or written the word *motherfucker*. This is clearly phony. On the other hand, there is a self-evident (if complicated) difference between the word *motherfucker* spoken in a kitchen and the same word broadcast over a loudspeaker. The neighbors of MOVE felt this difference, and most of Philadelphia officialdom agreed with them, if only in theory for the longest while.

The complications of this felt difference are certainly not trivial, and questions that emerged in this case regarding the legal standing as well as the cultural acceptability of the loudspeaker speeches were unevenly resolved. What legal scholar Paul Stern has written about the freedom-of-speech clause of the First Amendment indicates some of the liminal-like status of the public speech of MOVE (given MOVE's claim to be a political organization with a political aim): "On the continuum of private and public liberties designated in the First Amendment, freedom of speech stands somewhere in the middle—that is, somewhere between freedom of religious worship and freedom to petition the government for a redress of grievances."[49]

MOVE members did in turn assert their good neighborliness. Louise James and Laverne Sims testified ardently to the reciprocity of neighbors on Osage Avenue that included MOVE. Once again it is important they appealed to the old-fashioned contributions of an imagined small-town past: "The neighbors—I have read where the neighbors talked about how the MOVE people attacked them . . . But did the neighbors tell you, for example, how MOVE people baked bread for everybody . . . how when it snowed . . . MOVE members would get out early in the morning and they would shovel those walks."[50]

Class and Race on Osage Avenue

Class and race are complicated and slippery categories, as recent sociological and historical studies have elaborated.[51] Despite these studies Americans believe that they can identify differences of race fairly easily. Class is a more vexed categorical issue in the American popular mind. And when an event or a situation combines elements of class and race, all hell breaks loose, the uncertainties and anxieties of our variously stratified society coming to the surface. Surely this was the case with MOVE on Osage Avenue. Just the basic facts of the story suggest such entanglings—a Northeast city in the 1980s, having lost its industrial base and the production jobs that went with it, a reliance on information and service industries, a predominantly black, homeowning neighborhood in West Philadelphia, a predominantly black, anti-system group with a goal of getting its members out of jail and an ideological physiognomy that was impossible to pin down, black elected city officials, a white business community, white "frontline" commissioners of police and fire forces.

Charting the precipitates of such entanglings shows how the situations get named by and for the public. For such naming indicate more general attitudes about the possibilities of life—and life-styles—in specific times and places.

For example, it is illuminating to follow the descriptions of the 6200 block of Osage Avenue in the mass media. The leading daily newspaper, The *Philadelphia Inquirer*, slides around categories of class and property in its attempts to pin down what kind of neighborhood MOVE moved into: May 2, "working-class neighborhood"; May 5, "traditional working-class neighborhood"; May 9, "middle-class neighborhood"; May 10, "block of row houses . . . of teachers, nurses, janitors, police officers has worked hard to enter the middle class"; May 13, "house-proud, middle-class, stable community"; May 15, "what once had been an ordinary row house in a stable working-class West Philadelphia community."

Clearly the editorial board of the newspaper did not sit down and decide, one day, to fix its vision of the class nature of the block. Only academics and revolutionaries are inclined toward such definition mongering. But the looseness and variability of these class labels is revealing and suggests some questions that would require a comparative analysis to answer. Could it be that black neighborhoods that have not been subject to the decimation of economic dislocation and familial disruption, elaborated by such researchers as William Julius Wilson and Elijah Anderson in their compelling studies, are hard for the establishment media, the politicians, and the very residents to get into focus? Could it be simply that in the United States class is so loose a concept that, short of extreme poverty and extreme wealth, it is very difficult to gauge a neighborhood's exact class location? Could it be that, in the efforts to portray the Osage Avenue block as normal, there was some discursive confusion about the ramifications of the respective categories of working-class and middle-class: working-class implying steadiness, a work ethic, tradition, and solidarity; middle-class implying professionalism, property ownership, and status? I can only suggest these possibilities. What is clear is that the lack of fixity reflected some conflicts about precisely what the neighborhood was and, according to some commentators, what should be done. Ms. F, an African-American interviewed in the American Friends Service Committee's survey, articulated some of the points of tension around the general issues of class mobility and status.

> I understand, being Black, how much emphasis people put on being in a nice neighborhood. That fight is still going on in the Black community. There are friends of mine in Mt. Airy who say Goode didn't have a choice and they brought it on themselves. These are the same people who grew up with me at 25th and Diamond, who moved on up and participated in demonstrations so that people could not move into apartment buildings because it would lower their . . . real estate value. That fight, to be respectable . . . to be . . . upwardly mobile and separate yourselves from the riff and the raff and the people who embarrass you or drag the race down . . . is very much a part of this whole discussion about MOVE for the Black community.[52]

A Temple University professor of political science gave a similar assessment of this issue when he spoke of the Osage Avenue residents' general attachment to property values.[53] But on the other side, community activist and organic mediator Novella Williams characterized the neighbors in the following way: On May 12, "I saw the neighbors leaving with their small plastic bags, not Gucci bags, just plain old plastic bags. Just ordinary people unknown to all of us at that time."[54] Similarly, the neighbors themselves characterized their block as a "small working class block" in their letter to Governor Thornburgh.

Perhaps what emerges as a constant out of all this oscillation in class determination is the simultaneous impulses to portray the block as sympathetic and *absolutely* normal and to constrict this portrayal by the persistent use of diminutive terms, even when the class characterization is elevated from working to middle. "Tidy," "stable," and "small," "traditional," "row houses," and "worked hard to enter" all compress the image and make of the block almost a miniature painting—perfect and manageable and precious and yet, as became the case, easily lost. Such ultimate abandonment is indeed the hidden peril of the sentimental discourse, crying alligator tears as the pure souls ascend to heaven.

Along with the implications of class, the ways that Osage Avenue was represented had implications of race. Philadelphia, like all major U.S. cities, has experienced racial conflicts at various levels of institutions. Mayor Goode had as recently as March 1985 presented to the City Council a hotly debated city budget that some read to be punishing the police and fire departments for their sluggishness in raising the percentages of minorities on these forces. The Urban League report of 1985 speaks at several points to the issue of minority representation in the police force and to the goal of greater responsiveness on the part of the police department to the concerns of the black community. Further, in the week of April 11, 1985, the police operation "Cold Turkey" had resulted in mass arrests of minorities in the attempt to catch drug traffickers. Both the city Law Department and the ACLU signed a consent decree prohibiting such types of arrests.

Despite this background of institutional racial conflict, the MOVE problem was never primarily represented as being about race. After all, Mayor Goode was African-American, the residents of Osage Avenue were African-American, MOVE was African-American. How could this confrontation be about race? A few voices, both during and after the confrontation, questioned the putting aside of the issue of race, and these voices became powerful enough to enter the official findings of the MOVE commission report (although not unanimously for the commissioners). The following paragraph appeared in the "Additional Comments" section, emerging out of a report that does not in any way insist upon a reading of the conflict as being about race. "The commission believes that the decisions of various city officials to permit construction of the bunker, to allow the use of high explosives and, in a 90-minute period, the firing of at least 10,000 rounds of ammunition at the house, to sanction the dropping of a bomb on an occupied row house and to let a fire burn in a row house occupied by children would not have been made had the MOVE house and its occupants been situated in a comparable white neighborhood" (p. 69). Why did this comment surface in a report that had largely ignored race as a factor? Is it so difficult to sustain a discussion of race in a city that, by electing an African-American mayor, believes it has successfully resolved racial issues? Is it also difficult to articulate exactly how an issue could be about race when so many of the protagonists, on all sides, were of the same race? One local African-American congressman, Lucien Blackwell, went back and forth on this question. In the seventies he believed MOVE was being harassed by the police and that it was "a 'racial' problem." Then, invited to a Powelton Village residents' meeting, he was surprised to see that "most of the people there were black people, just ordinary black people and for the first time I realized that it was not a racial problem with MOVE but that it was something else that I just did not understand."[55] Finally, Blackwell did protest, at a May 7, 1985, meeting with the mayor, that something would have been done earlier for the residents of Osage Avenue if it had been a white neighborhood.

Indeed, if race played no role in the fate of the neighborhood and of MOVE on May 13, 1985, why did police tell all the whites in the large crowd watching the event unfold in the area of the burning Osage Avenue to leave? The only reason to make such a distinction is that someone involved in the situation was naming it and reacting to it as being about race. Perhaps the final word in this section should go to Gerald Renfrew, block captain of Osage Avenue, who, four years after the confrontation, faced an audience at an American Friends Service Committee Human Rights Day Forum and said, "Blacks in this city have no rights, we are not recognized as human beings."[56]

What Is Normal?

Hannah Arendt wrote that "it is decisive that society, on all its levels, excludes the possibility of action . . . Instead, society expects from each of its members a certain kind of behavior, imposing innumerable and various rules, all of which tend to 'normalize' its members, to make them behave, to exclude spontaneous action or outstanding achievement."[57]

Thus for Arendt the normal is opposed to action. Harvey Sacks, while perhaps he would have agreed with Arendt's notions of the conformity and constriction in being normal, asserted that normal, or ordinary, has to be accomplished. It's a job to do "being ordinary." "Whatever you may think about what it is to be an ordinary person in the world, an initial shift is not [to] think of 'an ordinary person' as some person, but as somebody having as one's job, as one's constant pre-occupation, doing 'Being ordinary' . . . you might want to check out the costs of venturing into making your life an epic."[58]

Forced to do "being ordinary" for a public audience, the Osage Avenue neighbors and intermittently MOVE itself came up with the lineaments of an ordinary life. They were asked, however implicitly, to articulate the dimensions of ordinariness, of normalcy. Clifford Bond, referring to the sense he had of his options in dealing with MOVE, stated: "I didn't have too many choices, as a citizen, as a homeowner, as a parent."[59] This role-divided and role-defined self was portrayed as having limited Bond. In accomplishing it, his action was constrained. Similarly, Cassandra Carter spoke of her sense of a normal life: "I left under the impression that I could come back to a home with some sort of damage and I could have my insurance company put my window back and I would be able to have friends over to visit and get on with a normal life like anybody living in Germantown or West Oak Lane or even in South Philly or, say 52nd Street."[60]

Carter cited all of these locations of normalcy in the city. These lives are *not* being presented as epics. They pare down the action—having friends over to visit, cooking meals, making Santa Claus. I believe it is a real question as to whether this is too much or too little to ask for in our society. Who automatically gets such things? Which individuals are watched to make sure they are accomplishing these things and no other things?

On this last point, Michel Foucault has written much. The broad process of normalization has engaged many mechanisms to scrutinize behavior of everyday life: "a whole micro-penalty of time (lateness, absences, interruptions of tasks), of activity (inattention, negligence, lack of zeal), of behavior (impoliteness, disobedience), of speech (idle chatter, insolence), of the body (incorrect attitudes, irregular gesture, lack of cleanliness), of sexuality (impurity, indecency)."[61]

Indeed, many of the questions put to Birdie/Michael concerned who ate what, who cleaned what in the MOVE house. Similarly, the neighbors brought forth a highly detailed account of their daily lives, even when not asked to overtly or assiduously. Clearly, some in society are, for reasons of class, race, or politics, closer to an edge of normalcy, and they are more often asked to perform their normalcy for the judging dominant culture: "The child, the patient, the criminal are known in infinitely more detail than are the adult, the healthy individual and the law abiding citizen."[62] Were the adult law-abiding neighbors of MOVE suspect, even minimally, because of their geographical proximity to MOVE, and therefore did they need to do "being ordinary" to an even greater degree than usual? Or did they perform these roles so actively because the dominant culture has a difficult time reading *ordinary* and *African-American* together?

Finally, the detailing, scrutinizing knife that Foucault identifies as *the* modality of disciplinary power in our modern age is one that can slice both ways. It can create categories of the abnormal, the criminal, and the pathological, and, paradoxically, it can dissolve these same categories. This latter process occurred in the MOVE commission hearings during the strange and unsettling testimony of the forensic pathologist, Ali Hameli. Hameli, with slides and accompanying text, minutely examined the X rays and other records of the MOVE members, adults and children both, who perished in the fire. A strange thing occurs as he elaborates on old bone scars from a broken clavicle or an indication of a tooth extraction or even an appendectomy scar. After all the talk of MOVE's profanity, violence, and primitivity, these homely details of doctor and dentist visits, of bodies shaped and reshaped by the tools of modern medicine, make the members of MOVE themselves seem more mundane and full of the pathos of ordinariness. In this way, the modern genre of the dossier, which, according to Dreyfus and Rabinow, has replaced the epic, can actually bring a sentimentalizing discourse a bit more down to the tragic earth.

CHAPTER FOUR

Bureaucratic Discourse
The Policy, the Plan, the Operation

It is true that the Expert is growing more common in this society, to the point of becoming its generalized figure, distended between the exigency of a growing specialization and that of a communication that has become all the more necessary. . . . But
his success is not so terribly spectacular. In him, the productivist law that requires a
specific assignment (the condition of efficiency) and the social law that requires circulation (the form of exchange) enter into contradiction.

Michel de Certeau, *The Practice of Everyday Life*

Already I feel a great sleepiness coming over me. Is this the nature of
political bureaucracy, to induce an ultimate sluggishness in the client
(or analyst in this case)? It is true that as clients and constituents we
regard bureaucracies in general as monolithic, impenetrable, impersonal and thick. I want to explore the relationship between this common-
sense response to the notion of bureaucracy and the classical theoretical
statements about bureaucracy. A finely grained analysis of the discourse
of a bureaucracy in action reveals how the bureaucratic social mind can
and cannot engage its constituent's reality.

Before I elaborate the elements of bureaucracy as laid out in classical
and contemporary theory, I want to say something more about discursive interdependency. In its broader stretch, this study explores not simply the dominant discourses of social and political conflicts nor simply
the copresence of subordinate discourses in these situations, but rather
the interrelationships between the dominant and the subordinate discourses. Such interrelationships, methodologically gauged via the textual exegeses of discourse analysis, are the bearers of socially
unconscious conflicts about the way institutions conceptualize and attempt to communicate and control their own and other's humanity.

The bureaucratic discourse dominated the city administration for the duration of the MOVE conflict (somewhat arbitrarily dated 1980–85, the years of Wilson Goode as managing director in the Green administration and then as mayor). Further, the sentimental discourse, detailed in chapter 3, interacted with the bureaucratic in important and meaningful ways. This may appear an odd coupling, as those in charge developed a plan to remove MOVE from Osage Avenue. The fact that these two discourses seem to be so antithetical, their assumptions about language, the body, interpersonal relationships, and emotion so different, actually bolsters the claim of interdependency rather than denies it. Ultimately, the bureaucrat needs to present a heart to a public that never fully accepts the premises of bureaucracy, and since a heart does not come with the territory, it must be imported from another sphere. Simon Dentith makes a similar point about the burgeoning hard-science discourse of the nineteenth century: "Political Economy was always to be an inadequate discourse, either reinforced or tempered by other, heterogeneous, discourses—religion or nationalism, or historicism or Romantic organicism."[1] Within a pluralistic context, no one discourse can ever fully stand alone.

In the MOVE conflict it was not just the bureaucratic discourse's inability to claim or articulate the more personal, "human" visions of social life that made it dependent on an alternative discourse. It was also the pervasive error and malfunction in the bureaucratic language and mechanisms themselves. The MOVE conflict was littered with lost memos and plans, misfiled reports, uncertainties as to what constituted code violations, incomplete notes of meetings stuffed into trouser pockets, and ambiguities about the chain of command. Such chronic dysfunctioning reveals a bureaucratic impulse thwarted or stymied by systemic lack of control and can tell us about bureaucracy's (in)capacity for dealing with both chronic and acute conflicts. In terms of the specific contours and limitations of bureaucratic discourse, I am interested in how the discourse gets bent as it attempts to describe such pervasive dysfuntioning. Once again, we shall see a necessary borrowing and importation of other discourses in the service of these descriptions and explanations.

It matters not whether the participants in the conflict consciously and strategically mixed and matched their discourses in recognition of the logical and normative limits of sayability in one or another discourse or whether some unconscious process of discursive sorting operated to the same end. The important thing is that specific worldviews either do or do not get brought to bear in the actions taken around social conflicts. Further, among those worldviews that are represented, some predominate over others. The goal here is to explore the contours of the discourses that do represent and construe an event, to explore the interactions of the extant discourses, and to mark the absences of those discourses unspoken or unacknowledged.

Weber's Classical Theory of Bureaucracy

The sociologist Max Weber was very interested in the organizational assumptions and prerequisites of bureaucracy. Writing in the very early years of the twentieth century, he viewed bureaucracy as a contemporary organizational form that was in the process of augmenting its purview and power. In his analyses of bureaucracy he constructed a typology of bureaucratic organization. He outlined the following central conditions: (1) bureaucracies are organized along hierarchical lines, with an administrative division of labor; (2) authority is distributed in a stable manner, (3) there are fixed and official jurisdictional areas ordered by codified rules; (4) regulation of matters is abstract, not handled on a case-by-case basis; (5) bureaucrats have generally regulated qualifications, training, examinations, and expertise; (6) official activity is understood as something distinct from the sphere of private life.[2] Weber's analysis covered both the structural elements of bureaucratic institutions and the social-psychological profile of the bureaucratic incumbent, at least in terms of his or her official persona. This combination of the structural and the social-psychological is important to my analysis of the discourse of the bureaucrats in the MOVE case.

Weber had an ambivalent attitude toward bureaucracy. On the one hand he found it had a "purely technical superiority over any other form of organization."[3] On the other hand he worried about the accessibility of bureaucracy to a variety of political and economic interests and ideologies, as well as its general curtailment of individual freedom. With the latter in mind, Weber explored the paradoxical relationship (as he saw it) of bureaucracy to democracy. As he put it, "Democracy as such is opposed to the 'rule' of bureaucracy, in spite and perhaps because of its unavoidable yet unintended promotion of bureaucracy."[4] As I understand it, Weber is referring to the theoretically open, achievement-based positions of bureaucracies, an openness encouraged and sought by ascription-breaking democratic movements. Yet that rule of bureaucracy, once crystallized, is opposed to the dynamic change and openness of democracy. That action and change was viewed as deriving from the political sphere, a sphere wherein "the struggle for power and the promulgation of policy orients actions in a manner quite opposed to the bureaucratic orientation."[5] Politics is the source of policies, the kinds of actions in which ends are articulated. Bureaucracies deal almost exclusively with means.

One preliminary observation about the Philadelphia administration of Wilson Goode, as viewed through its actions in the MOVE conflict, is that it might best be described as having effected a strange and awkward combining of the bureaucratic and the political. This combining may have had something to do with the idiosyncrasies of the training and backgrounds of the protagonists, including Goode, who "has said that he learned more about management in the army than he did earning a master's degree in governmental administration at the University of Pennsylvania."[6] However, the proliferation of bureaucratic agencies in our society has tended in the direction of the bureaucratization of previous nonbureaucratic or antibureaucratic spheres of life. In asserting an infusion of the bureaucratic into the political, I am extending a point made by Kathy Ferguson, that "increasingly the social services and the police and military bureaucracies are merging, so that the two functions become inseparable; the poor are referred to the military for job 'training' and experience . . . the police are used to investigate welfare applicants to determine eligibility."[7] Recent studies of the relationship between bureaucracy and politics in Western democracies have spoken of an outright convergence of the two civic functions. Joel Aberbach et al. introduce the concept of the "pure hybrid": "The two roles have been converging—perhaps reflecting, as some have argued, a 'politicization' of the bureaucracy and a 'bureaucratization' of politics. [The pure hybrid] suggests speculatively that the last quarter of this century is witnessing the virtual disappearance of the Weberian distinction between the roles of the politician and the bureaucrat."[8]

This pure hybrid figure would then represent two previously distinct perspectives: the expert and the passionately committed. Such a convergence has distinct discursive ramifications. A question that may be asked of this case is, What does the infusion of policy issues into a bureaucratic discourse do to the issues and the discourse? Before attempting to answer this question, I take a closer look at the lineaments of the language of bureaucracy and at some contemporary critiques of bureaucratic organization itself.

Characteristics of Bureaucratic Language

Without a doubt, we know bureaucratic language when we hear it. It is commonly thought of as cumbersome, obscure, formulaic, distancing, and verbose. For example, when asked whether police forces in the future ought to drop an explosive from the air on a row house as a tactical feature of an operation, Police Commissioner Sambor replied: "I would think that as an absolute I would not consider it to be appropriate but that I would think that it would be a consideration within certain parameters, relative to testing and extensive knowledge as to what would be the results and the capacity of what was used."[9] There is no mistaking this answer. Its qualifications, variations on a theme, specifications, and references to experts, testing, and scientific experimentation all mark it as bureaucratic discourse.

Further, it is difficult, if not impossible, to locate individual responsibility in bureaucratic explanations of enacted procedures. This vanquishing of individual initiative and responsibility goes along with Weber's recognition of the normative splitting of the public and private selves of the bureaucrat. As such, bureaucratic discourse is a quintessentially public discourse. This is not the narrative-based public discourse prized and prescribed by Hannah Arendt. Rather it is the anonymous voice of that which Arendt termed "the rule of no-one." The public-private split, along with the other criteria of the bureaucratic organization (hierarchy, rule-boundedness, universalism), creates a condition of severe constraints on what kind of statements can be made. Jean-François Lyotard in *The Postmodern Condition* discusses the classes of statements possible in institutional contexts: "[Institutions] also privilege certain classes of statements (sometimes only one) whose predominance characterizes the discourse of the particular institution: there are things that should be said, and there are ways of saying them. Thus: orders in families, questions in philosophy, performativity in businesses. Bureaucratization is the outer limit of this tendency" (p. 17).

As I am interested in hybrid or contaminated discourses, those combining features of more than one institutional language, it is important to consider what happens when the bureaucratic discourse is combined with another. Claire Lerman's analysis of what she calls the "institutional voice" (IV) provides an example of what the bureaucratic discourse sounds like when combined with a discourse of moral virtue. She claims that you get "a system of language and interactive structures through which speakers distance themselves from personally responsible 'I' statements (in many forms) and from a given topic . . . As the selfless personification of power and tradition, the IV has an inherent claim to virtue, a recurrent theme of its topics. Therefore, the IV uses the language of morality for the discourse of power."[10]

Below we will hear what the forced coupling of bureaucratic and sentimental discourses sounds like. And we will be able to oppose the kinds of things it can articulate to the kinds of things it cannot.

Critiques of Bureaucracy and of the Classical Theory of Bureaucracy

Contemporary critiques of bureaucracy as a form of social organization as well as critiques of the Weberian analyst of bureaucracy center on approximately four main points. First, several critics draw attention to the dysfunctions of bureaucratic systems and, a related matter, to internal conflicts within systems. Peter Blau argues this point: "What is missing [from Weber's account of bureaucracy] is a . . . systematic attempt to specify the dysfunctions of the various elements and to examine the conflicts that arise between the elements comprising the system . . . Selznick has emphasized that the formal structure is only one aspect of the actual social structure and that organizational members interact as whole persons and not merely in terms of the formal roles they occupy."[11]

Blau's point about internal conflict is tied to a second point, attributed to Selznick, regarding the impossibility of total bureaucratic self-splitting. Interacting as whole persons within organizations, the bureaucrats must engage in particularistic and "irrational" behaviors. Beyond the fact of individual interest anticipating and/or emerging from internal organizational conflicts, there is the empirical and logical problem of the impossibility of categorically separating subjectivity and objectivity. Gerald E. Frug makes this point: "Objectivity is usually associated with the ideas of impersonality or commonness rather than with those of the self—with the perspective of universality rather than that of particularity. But any reference to what we share collectively must take into account each of the individual components that make up the collectivity. There can no more be universal, collective, or shared goals separate from the particular goals advanced by specific people, than there can be an objective world of nature separate from the individual features of the world sought to be described."[12]

Contemporary analysts of bureaucracy such as Donald Levine have clarified the Weberian analysis of bureaucracy by specifying the precise types of rationality featured in bureaucratic forms of organization. Levine notes that both the instrumental and the formal types of rationality predominate in bureaucracy. He quotes Weber's characterization of the instrumental form as "the methodical attainment of a particular given practical end through the increasingly precise calculation of adequate means." About formal rationality, Levine writes that it entails "a methodical ordering of activities through the establishment of fixed rules and routines."[13]

It seems to me that the appearance of the instrumental form of rationality in bureaucracies leads, inevitably and logically, to a severing of the process of considering ends from the process of considering means.[14] Levine indicts instrumental rationality as having an "eroding effect on moral authority and the bases of moral community."[15] Thus the third point to keep in mind about bureaucracies is the tendency to pay excessive attention to means to the detriment of whatever ends have been prescribed from some other sphere.

Finally, Kathy Ferguson makes the point that bureaucracies have an aversion to uncertainty and yet are unable to eliminate it. Rules, regulations, and universalism all presume a stability of roles and actions. Such a presumption must affect not only the role of the bureaucrat but also the personae of clients and constituencies. Ferguson writes: "Like the administrators who staff bureaucracies, clients who receive the goods and services issuing from bureaucracies are required to attend constantly to the image which they present to the organization, to engage in successful impression management . . . to modify their own behavior accordingly, or be denied crucial services . . . bureaucracies claim to operate on the basis of rules, which are neutral, objective and scientific, while clients are seen as operating on the basis of values, which are personal, subjective, and biased."[16]

These four critical elaborations of some of the perhaps hidden features of bureaucracy—dysfunction, impossibility of self-splitting, excessive instrumentality, and inability to process or eliminate uncertainty—are key to an understanding of the expression of bureaucracy in the MOVE conflict. They help to illuminate both the decisions taken by those in charge and the discursive characterizations of these decisions during and after the confrontation.

Policies, Plans, and Operations: Of Commands Unchained

Policies

Mayor Wilson Goode claimed that he had "inherited" a general policy toward MOVE from the previous administration of William Green. This policy was characterized as "hands-off" and meant that police would stay at the corner of 62nd Street and Osage Avenue, rather than come down the block to the MOVE house; that License and Inspection employees would refrain from inspecting the metamorphosing house; that water and electricity services would be continued to the MOVE house long after bills had stopped being paid. This policy developed in a legal atmosphere that, up to late 1984, declared that "most sustainable charges [against MOVE members] are misdemeanors." Nevertheless, the final report of the MOVE commission characterized Mayor Goode's policy as "one of appeasement, non-confrontation and avoidance." And point 3 of the report elaborated on this by claiming that, "with this policy of benign avoidance, the Mayor hoped that the problem might dissipate on its own, particularly, that MOVE would weary of unanswered challenges, modulate their confrontational behavior and/or relocate. To a great extent, then, MOVE effectively paralyzed the normal functioning of city government, as it applied to MOVE and to the Osage neighborhood" (p. 22).

The juxtaposition and casual association of the words *benign* and *paralyzed* in this paragraph from the report give a good idea of the paradox of the confrontation between the bureaucracy of the City of Philadelphia and the MOVE group. Something is benign when it is not harmful or aggressive; it leaves the relevant system alone. There is no sense of willful antipathy or hostility. It is a soft and pleasant word. Paralysis is obviously more serious. The system is frozen, incapable of action, essentially dead. So how could something benign lead to paralysis? This is indeed the question at the heart of the relationship between bureaucracy and crisis.

One possible avenue for answering this question is to explore the issue of how Goode and his subordinates came to understand this policy. Was it, as one might assume, written down in a directive or official memo from the mayor? Here is the mayor's response to this question.

We did not have any meetings where in fact I said to Department heads, "This is a policy which you are to follow in terms of 6221 Osage Avenue." However, it was a policy which [was] clearly understood by them to be the policy, and therefore I did not see any need at all to further pursue a written policy or to further pursue the clarification of that policy in view of the fact that my major concern was that none of these departments would send out to the streets, to Osage Avenue, any personnel that could in fact be put in danger, that the only time they would go out would be as part of a comprehensive program that would come forth from the Managing Director's or the Mayor's office.[17]

Here Goode gave a situated-meaning answer—"You had to have been there. The context specified." Such an answer is not atypical of witnesses in inquisitional settings, as Molotch and Boden have shown in their study of the Watergate hearings.[18] However, it is a curious answer coming from someone who was in charge of a vast city bureaucracy of welfare and law-enforcement agencies. Goode seems to be reflecting a process of communication more appropriate to a small-scale, informal organization. The MOVE commissioners were stymied by this free-floating policy, and they asked Managing Director Brooks how, as Goode's point man on MOVE, he came to understand it. "A. And it was both in a nondirect way, meaning a tacit kind of approval, as well as by some implications that we would not create a confrontation with MOVE . . . Q. Was it a conscious decision, sir, to have this policy developed tacitly as opposed to nontacitly, or did it just happen? A. I did not get it in writing, and I only communicated it either in a declarative sentence or in some other kind of a statement to no more than two or three people. There was no great promulgation of an order."[19]

While I write this, I always have the image of the burning houses on May 13 at the back of my mind. I think this is important and not incidental. You see, I am struggling to find some path from Goode's policy, and the way that policy was communicated, to that fire. Perhaps this a futile enterprise—too many lines of causality to portray in a more or less linear type of analysis. But the bureaucratic repression (not the same thing as repressive bureaucracy) that would codify its policy, not officially, but only "nondirectly," "tacitly," with "implications" and, at the most, scarcely believable "declarative sentences," must speak to the larger question of bureaucracy's relation to crisis. Before leaving these explanations by Goode and Brooks, I want to draw even closer attention to their language. Both tend to circle back to points they have just made, making them again with slightly different words. Both tend to be abstract in the main but have moments of anticipated concreteness that seem to erupt out of the speeches. Thus the reference at the end of Goode's answer to a "program" that would come out of the managing director's or the mayor's office, and the putative "promulgation of an order" in Brooks's response. The testimony of these witnesses has a marked tendency to point a way to something concrete to move beyond indirection, but it is almost always to something that never actually occurred.

At the other end of this tacitly understood policy were the Osage Avenue residents who could not get ambulances to come down their street when they were ill and could not get police to make direct interventions in their altercations with MOVE members. Thus the bureaucracy simply shut itself down, as the MOVE commission report asserts, when it came to the constituents on Osage Avenue.

Caught in the middle of the policy and its "recipients" were those frontline workers, those whom Michael Lipsky has called "street-level bureaucrats." License and Inspection officer Rudolph Paliaga stated: "It was an unusual situation. And we deal with codes and ordinances. Criminal or potentially criminal matters are not within our jurisdiction. And as you can recall from previous testimony, the Police Department knew about the bunker. We are concerned with codes and ordinances."[20]

When one combines a nonarticulated policy of avoidance with the increasing specialization of functions of different agencies, and when one has as the nonobject of this inaction a group that confounds categorization through its continuous transgression of social boundaries, one has the feeling that the situation will either implode or explode. In fact, when the city solicitor for the Goode administration was asked whether she believed that civil enforcement remedies, remedies upon which political bureaucracies normally rely, would have worked in the MOVE case, she replied: "The civil enforcement remedies were not in my view any sort of—offered no real promises of solving the problem. They have been tried in the earlier period. They take an incredibly long time to develop and at the end of the process what you end up with are relatively minor fines or alternatively the prospect of having to enforce an injunction which brings you right back to the issue of how you deal with the confrontation or whether you wish to provoke the confrontation."[21]

There it is, the confrontation. It is always there, hovering in the back of bureaucratic discourse of the officials in charge. And there is no way to think beyond or, better yet, through this image from within that particular discourse.

Plans

Although he was widely perceived to be an energetic, detail-oriented administrator, when he decided the city should act against MOVE, Goode had minimal involvement in both the planning and the execution of the attack.

Jack Nagel, "Psychological Obstacles to Administrative Responsibility: Lessons
of the Move Disaster"

The plan was a good one. It could have worked. The fire was accidental, and was, in fact, unexpected. That does not, however, take away from the fact that we had a good plan that could have resulted in no loss of life nor property damage.

Wilson Goode, Press Conference, May 14, 1985

In the summer of 1984 the members of MOVE on Osage Avenue announced that they were going to hold a demonstration on August 8, the date of the sixth anniversary of the 1978 Powelton Village MOVE confrontation. It was at this point that policy evolved concretely into police. Mayor Goode, having designated Managing Director Brooks as the city official directly responsible for the MOVE conflict, concurred in Brooks's decision to turn the matter over to the police. Bennie Swans, executive director of the city's Crisis Intervention Network (a nonprofit agency to intervene and mediate situations of neighborhood violence) recounted a conversation he had with Brooks in the early summer of 1984: "The Managing Director indicated that he had reviewed the situation, that he had determined that the vehicle that he would use to resolve the problem with the MOVE organization was the police and that at this particular point all further civilian interaction was to cease and was, in fact, a police matter."[22]

What is so startling about this passage is the complete opposition that is being drawn between the police and civilian interaction. It is as if the possibility of some combination of the two is unthinkable and that once the police are brought into the picture, all notions of mediation, of community-based negotiation are negated. They inhabit different universes. Force and the threat of force drive out interactive speech.

Several other city agency officials were told essentially the same thing about this time, including the director of the Community Intervention Program and the assistant managing director of the city in charge of the Community Coordinating Committee. The police were viewed as essentially the "committee" of last resort. What is also true, however, is that the mayor and the managing director, both civilian representatives of authority, were considered to be at the top of the chain of command, even though MOVE had been designated a police matter. Thus the continuing relationship between the civilian bureaucracy and the police bureaucracy, in spite of the asserted theoretical gap between the two, created a paradoxical situation for those "in charge". This paradox subtends the discourse of these officials.

Thus in the summer of 1984 a police sergeant in the Bomb Disposal Unit was selected by the police commissioner to devise a plan. Sergeant Herbert Kirk did so without the benefit of a police department critique of the 1978 police action against MOVE, partly because Commissioner Sambor claimed to have become aware of such a critique only in June 1985 and partly because this critique was said to have been misfiled. The precise details of Kirk's 1984 plan were never completely revealed, as the one copy of the plan could not be located, according to Sambor.

These misfilings and misplacements are part of the general pattern of loss and error that emerges as one works through the archival history of the MOVE conflict. I consider below the possible meanings of such endemic dysfunctions. They seem to be linked to the bureaucratic dread of conflict, even when the bureaucracy at work is that of the police.

Although Sambor could not locate the written plan, he did recall his charge to Kirk: "The plan I wanted him to put together was to be one that was primarily a reactive one, that there was no intended assault . . . In that reactive posture, then we were to figure out a way to gain access to the premises for [tear] gas and smoke and to force the occupants out into the street."[23] Here again is a perplexing opposition between the alleged reactivity of the plan and the prescribed activity of injecting tear gas and smoke into the house and forcing the occupants out. This speech simply doesn't hold together, its beginning and end going off in different directions. Action and reaction are not the same things. Police are inclined to action. But given the background policy of nonconfrontation of the Goode administration, it is clear that any concrete plan that emerged from this environment would contain residues of notions of avoidance even as it asserted its impulse to act.

When August 8 came around, hundreds of police officers were sent to Osage Avenue. Neighbor children were evacuated. And nothing happened. Both the neighbors and the MOVE members were left pretty much where they had been before.

In the spring of 1985 Mayor Goode spelled out the criteria for a new plan that he wanted the police to develop. This plan was to draw together and address several issues that had been slowly congealing, including the possibility of arresting some of the MOVE members on specific criminal charges, the possibility of obtaining a court order to pick up and hold the children of the MOVE members, and the possibility of the neighbors of MOVE taking their own offensive action against MOVE, as they were threatening to do. It is interesting to note here, as Susan Wells does in her essay on the MOVE commission final report, that in the report Mayor Goode is deprived of a certain aggressive agency in the decision to develop a plan. Referring to point 9 ("More than any other factor, intensified pressure from the residents of Osage Avenue forced the mayor to abandon his policy of non-confrontation and avoidance, and to devise a strategy for resolving the problem quickly") Wells writes: "Since the mayor has been defined as passive and cautious, he can be excluded from initiating action; the formulation of a plan can be derived from neighborhood pressure rather than the mayor's decision . . . Activity, energy, and initiative are predicated elsewhere—to the neighbors, to the 'strategy,' or to those discussions that acknowledged the likelihood of death."[24] Wells's point here is that character is being constructed in the report to allow instrumental connections among events. I would agree with that but would go on to claim that the report simply mirrors the process whereby the bureaucratic discourse of the very protagonists themselves talked agency and causality into and out of existence through the course of the conflict.

At a meeting at the beginning of May 1985, Mayor Goode presented the following criteria to Police Commissioner Sambor for a plan

> that would enable us to make arrests of such MOVE members as the District Attorney was able to provide warrants for through a court order . . . #1, we wanted to make sure that the protection of police officers and firefighters and occupants of the house were paramount, that we did not want any loss of life. Secondly, we wanted him to handpick the officers who in fact would be in charge that day . . . We did not want people involved who may have a hot temper, who may have emotionally been attached to 1978 for some reason . . . [3] make sure we kept in mind at all times that there were children in the house. And we did not want to do anything that would harm the children inside the house . . . the Managing Director would—through the Department of Human Services and the Law Department would take whatever steps that he could in order to pick up the children in the park when they left home . . . The final point I gave to the Police Commissioner was: "Take your time. Prepare a good plan. And when you have the plan prepared, I want you to brief the Managing Director, who in turn will brief me. And we can then proceed with a tremendous amount of order."[25]

The outline form in which Goode presents his criteria for action has the outward appearance of bureaucratic narrative logic. Yet the plan-for-a-plan is really a series of ethical impulses entangled with logistical considerations. The sequence is revealing—first take care of the police and fire fighters, then worry about the history of the relations between police and MOVE, then take care of the children, then reverse the usual direction of the chain of command by briefing up rather than down the hierarchy. Finally, the word that closes the speech is one that takes on a great and troubled significance—*order*. Already, something trembles in that phrase, "a tremendous amount of order." It is as if the order threatens to fly apart, to reveal itself as a tenuously held together tremendum. As such, the phrase was prescient.

What then was the translation from the mayor's combined package of practical, deferential, and hortatory criteria to an actual tactical plan? The planning group designated by Sambor consisted of fairly low-ranking officers of the force, all three of whom were members of specifically strategic units of the police force. There was a lieutenant from the Bomb Disposal Unit, a sergeant who was a pistol instructor, and an officer who was a top sharpshooter. The particular units from which these planners came and the particular skills they brought to bear on their development of a plan are most significant. As Jack Greene has pointed out (personal communication), none of these officers were members of the more community-based Civil Affairs Division, and all had worked under Sambor before he became commissioner. Thus the closer one gets to the details of a plan for an operation against MOVE, the more purely tactical one gets and the lower one goes down the hierarchy.

As far as the plan itself was concerned, and what was actually known about it in advance of May 13, Brooks recapitulated the distinction, already noted, that had been effected between policy and police. Referring to police expertise and training, he answered a question about his knowledge of the tactical plan that was being developed: "No I wasn't [aware of the tactical details] . . . it would be my expectation that from an overall direction or plan that the Police Commissioner would make detailed subordinate plans for each element of his organization as they might be affected and for various and sundry kinds of activities that might occur."[26] Brooks did not know the details of the tactical plan and did not want to know, even though he was putatively in charge of the whole operation. He did not, could not, brief the mayor as to the plan. The gap between ends and means was ever widening. The language of his response evokes a sense of endless proliferation of details, details that are the inevitable product of any bureaucratic initiative, police or otherwise. And there is the sense that these details are burdens, foreign objects to be abjured. Thus was the plan for the May 13 MOVE operation developed, on the tactical ranges of the police department.

Operations

The operation of evacuating the neighborhood and attempting to serve arrest warrants on four of the MOVE members at 6221 Osage Avenue began early in the morning of May 13, 1985. In terms of foundational issues two concepts loomed large over the course of the operation. Both related to the bureaucratic organizational ideals of hierarchy and chain of command. The first concept was that of control. This covered a wide territory and included Goode's sense of being able or unable to control MOVE's actions in the early 1980s, the notion of a controlled operation, and the issue of controlled weapons' fire. The second concept was that of an order—who could give orders to whom, what constituted an order, and the variable relationships were between orders (or no orders) and actions.

With Mayor Goode not on the scene (he was in his home in the morning and in his City Hall office in the afternoon and evening) and Managing Director Brooks on the margins of the scene (he was in a local geriatric center a few blocks away) and with Police Commissioner Sambor and Fire Commissioner Richmond on the scene, the flow of information and directives was fragmented and mediated. These mediations via radio, telephones, and television screens were instrumental in shaping the workings out of such issues as control and the giving and taking of orders. Thus we must interrogate an event in which communication was not only structured according to specific discourses (here the bureaucratic and the military were dominant) but also facilitated or inhibited by electronic media of various kinds. These mediations were often faulty in their operations. For example, the police and fire departments' radios could not communicate with each other. Another example was Mayor Goode's belief, while watching the event unfold on television, that he saw water being hosed onto the burning MOVE house roof shortly after 6:00 P.M. This was not the case, and Goode later attributed this misperception to "snow" on his television screen. Such errors are symptomatic of bureaucracy's awkward relationship to conflict, crisis, and violence. It does and it doesn't want to know exactly what is going on in such situations.

CONTROL. Who was in control in the long relationship between the City of Philadelphia and MOVE? How did those individuals responsible for taking actions on behalf of the city alternatively deny or assert that they had control? And what did they mean by control?

In the early years of Goode's relationship with members of MOVE, the years in which he was managing director, he had as many as fifteen meetings with them. His characterizations of these meetings frequently involve his assessment of what kind of authority, control, and power he had vis-à-vis such things as his own schedule and what he could or should do for MOVE. MOVE members were requesting help to find a new home after the bulldozing of their Powelton Village house in 1978 and were beginning to lobby for the reopening of the cases of the nine MOVE members convicted and jailed for the killing of Officer Ramp. Goode represents his stance during the meetings in the following manner: "[I responded] that I did not have the power to do that and I was not aware of the facts or the circumstances surrounding 1978 . . . And the meetings as they went on became progressively more hostile when they determined that I would listen but basically, as they said, not respond, not act or not use my position, use my power to right the wrong that had been committed against them." Finally, after Goode did put them in touch with some city agencies that were responsible for housing, but continued to refuse to act on the convicted MOVE members issue, he began to decline to meet with them. He explains his own change: "They would call and set a time and date to be at my office for me to meet with them at that time and date. I declined because I wanted to control my schedule and not have them do so."[27]

In these passages action and inaction intermingle and separate in uneasy ways. At some points power is linked to knowledge (of facts and circumstances). At other points power seems to reside in the position, to be deployed or not at will. At these points the bureaucratic authority absorbs but does not respond. This representation of withheld action seems almost perverse. It is not exactly willful, not exactly structural, rather something in between. There is a tension between the requisites of a position and some unarticulated desire to be, perhaps, available, neutral, benign, and paralyzed at the same time. Finally, with control an issue in this situation, Goode seems to be reduced to controlling his own schedule, schedules clearly being a key point of power in the asymmetrical relationship between bureaucrats and clients. There is both pathos and bravado in this image of controlling one's schedule. The articulation of this seemingly minor point in the MOVE hearings attests to how important the notion of control was.

The emergence of control as an issue for Goode was not confined to his direct dealings with MOVE (which essentially ended in the summer of 1982). It also arose in his general response to the neighbors of MOVE on Osage Avenue, which he characterized in the following way: "Anytime any group, which is a terrorist group, decides that it wants to go into a neighborhood, to, in essence, hold that whole neighborhood hostage, and ask in return for releasing that neighborhood, the release of persons from prisons who have been sentenced by a judge over which the Mayor has no control. There is very little anyone can do with that."[28] Goode's representation of his own powers insists that they ran up against two brick walls, the wall of terrorism (all the fears of unpredictable violence, ferocity, irrationality, etc.) and the wall of the division of administrative labor (judges judge, mayors create budgets, etc.). Both walls deprived him of control and seemed to isolate him in a space between the forces of violence and excess and the forces of legitimate coercion. How indeed, when looked at in this way, could he evoke a secular, truly political reading of power?

It is now the time to look directly at the theory and practice of political bureaucracy's relationship to violence. I don't think that the public can sustain and live with the knowledge that politics is innately about "the monopoly of legitimate force over a given territory," that politicians, as Weber so magnificently elaborated, must involve themselves with the forces of darkness.[29] And indeed, as Machiavelli, Weber, and Gramsci, among others, have noted, the modern state does not have to and does not in fact continuously apply force over its territory. The state has other means available to it. So it is easy to forget the crucial link and to view state-sponsored violence over those in its won territory as episodic accidents, necessary evils against criminal foes, or, when the violence is clearly elaborate, monumental, and excessive, as aberrations. Because it does seem a leap from the bureaucracy of political administration with its memos and meetings and scheduling tugs-of-war to antitank guns and tear gas and military explosives brought to bear on a neighborhood. And the leap is effected through a mixing of the language of bureaucracy and that of warlike violence. Let me provide a particularly telling example of the tense yet inevitable cohabiting of these two discourses in the characterization of "legitimate" violence by legitimate officials. This time the former police commissioner of Philadelphia is testifying about the beating of a MOVE member as he came out of the Powelton Village house in 1978. "I noted that there was some kind of a fracas behind the armored vehicle and sent someone over to see what it was about. Apparently when he came out of the house our personnel who were over there believed that he had a knife in his hand. And subsequently he was clobbered and subdued."[30] *Clobbered* comes from one universe of human relations, *subdued* from another. Cavemen and bullies on the playground clobber each other. Parents and psychiatrists subdue their charges. Brute force on one side, calm control on the other. What are they doing in the same sentence? There is no irony here, no self-critical play of images. The clobbering simply erupts from the bureaucratic language of armored vehicles and personnel and subduings. Such eruptions are inevitable leakings out of alternative worldviews when these worldviews collide and commingle in real life.

Police characterizations of the May 13 operation also expressed real preoccupation about control. Here control was understood as carrying out a controlled operation. Police Commissioner Sambor addressed the issue of control in his opening statement to the MOVE commission: "The plan for May 13 was the most conservative, disciplined and safe operation which we could devise based upon these [1978] lessons. They called for the use of water, smoke and gas to drive the occupants into the street where they could be dealt with in a legal, safe and public manner . . . Police gunfire was to be directed on command only and only at confirmed MOVE shooters. Indeed, throughout the day police were presented with opportunities to shoot MOVE members but held their fire."[31] These words, "conservative, disciplined and safe," "on command only," conjure up a violence qualified and constrained by all of civilization's dicta about the use of legitimate force. This action was to be, and according to this testimony was actually controlled. Yet the hovering images of burning houses, ten thousand rounds of police gunfire, and explosives blowing off the porches of neighboring houses persist and mock the presentation. Any constraint—police officers who, in the midst of this inferno, held their fire—becomes the magnified covering image. When questioned specifically about this apparent contradiction between image and reality, police officers posited organizational preconditions to deny the contradiction. Those who were trained in the specifics of the tactical tasks at hand were supervising those tasks. Thus there must have been control. Expertise is both a necessary and sufficient condition for controlled functioning. A stake-out inspector was asked, "Just how much control was there as it turns out? A. Well, there was a Stake-Out trained supervisor with each one of these teams. The only way I can answer your question in terms of high-ranking officers being with these individual teams that those officers did not possess Stake-Out training. So consequently they weren't put or wouldn't be put with the Stake-Out officers to direct them. Stake-Out officers were with their own supervisors is what I am trying to say, who were trained."[32] Randall Collins has written on a kind of violence unique to bureaucracies: "The large-scale and remote organizational forms of modern society do not eliminate the tools of violence and manipulation, but only depersonalize them. Turning from the evil of ferocity, modern social structure delivers us into the hands of another evil: callousness."[33] In the MOVE case we find in the words and in the deeds of those bureaucratic officials in charge a complicated mixture of ferocity and callousness.

ORDERS. In the ideal typical situation of a strict hierarchy, strict rules of command, codified job descriptions, and a division between public and private personae, an order is a perfectly reasonable and unproblematic type of action for a superior to take vis-à-vis a subordinate. In the real world of bureaucratic interactions, things are a lot murkier. The MOVE case highlights the phenomenology of the speech act known as an order in a singular way. In spite of an asserted chain of command that for this operation put the managing director in charge of the oversight of the plan and the police commissioner in charge of the tactical aspects of the plan, there were numerous complications, both organizational and situational. Mayor Goode was still at the putative top of the hierarchy. The fire department was also involved and somehow slipped into and out of the interstices of the chain of command. Various mediations shaped and interrupted the communications among those on and off the scene. What is interesting for our purposes is how these complications infused the discourse of the operation and the articulated formulations of the protagonists, as actions either were or were not taken.

Let me focus on the controversial question of who could and did order the fire department to put out the fire that started on the MOVE house roof pursuant to the dropping of the explosives on that roof. The bomb[34] was dropped at 5:27 P.M. after a daylong battle in which tear gas, water, explosives, and gunfire had all been ineffective in forcing the MOVE members out of their house. The stated purpose of the bomb was to eliminate the bunker that had been built on the roof. Rather than eliminating the bunker, however, the explosives ignited a fire, probably by coming into contact with a barrel of gasoline that was stored there. At 5:49 P.M. the helicopter pilot reported seeing flames on the roof of the house. The "squirts" of the Philadelphia Fire Department were turned on for the first time at 6:32 P.M. Conventional fire fighting began at 9:30 P.M. By next morning, the entire block of Osage Avenue was completely destroyed, and all eleven people in the MOVE house were dead.

In the case of the burning of the MOVE house and the entire block, the combination of will to absolute control and the impossibility of control infused the epistemological uncertainties regarding orders and decision making. This combination simultaneously took bureaucratic rationalism to uncontrollable extremes of internal subdivision and let loose an anarchy where individual police and fire fighters acted on their own.

The day began with the fire department's large and powerful squirt guns being used as offensive weapons in the attempt to flush out the MOVE members. At about 11:15 A.M., these streams of water were shut down. When asked about the precise interaction between police and fire fighters in this moment of decision making, Fire Commissioner Richmond said: "I don't know that request [to shut them down] is the word. I don't know that order is the word. But it was at their desire that we shut these down." Later in his testimony, Richmond was asked how the chain of command worked during the time of the fire itself. "Q. Let me ask you the general question, then. What was your understanding as to who could instruct the Fire Department to turn the water on and to turn the water off? A. Well, I will say this in response to that, that I am fully responsible for any Deputy Commissioner, any Deputy Chief, any Battalion Chief or company officer or firefighter who turned off a hose line at the bequest, the instruction, the request, the insinuation of a police officer . . . When we knew we had a fire . . . we had water to the gates of the squirts, meaning they were ready to go upon order."[35]

Here, speech acts fly fast and furiously. They include requests, bequests, instructions, orders, and even, an elusive one, insinuations. Richmond cannot exactly say what this thing was that was transmitted from the police to the fire department. He seems clear on his own internal hierarchy, but the interaction of these two bureaucracies fogs the conceptualization. This hyperactive definition deployment is, partly a function of slippage in clarity of hierarchy and partly a function of bureaucratic discourse's exfoliating properties, its ability to break things down into minute details and therefore to get lost in them.

Richmond also makes reference to the conflict of interest enmeshed within the decision to fight or not fight the fire. He notes that turning the squirts back on the roof could knock over any police officer who had managed to get onto it. He notes that the water could also decrease the visibility of police and fire fighters on the street and in the alley and cause them to be targets of people shooting from within the MOVE house. In this line of thought, Richmond is articulating a seemingly straightforward precedent from the 1960s. According to fire-fighting consultant Charles King, in that period of "civil unrest" (King's term) "more firemen were shot, injured and killed by gunfire than police . . . Almost all of your major cities, including Philadelphia, either philosophically or in a directive determined that in a riot or in an unrest, that was a police department situation . . . Once that's contained, the fire department assumes a subordinate role."[36] The questions that remain, however, are, How is it determined that one is in a riot situation? and How do the lines of command and coordination shift when the fire department is a part of both the tactical operation and the support services operation?

How, in fact, did the police commissioner see the same situation? His is an assertion of collaboration.

It was at that time [5:55] that the Fire Commissioner and I were at the vicinity of 62nd and Osage, that I asked the Fire Commissioner that 'If

we let the the fire burn to get the bunker, could we control the fire?'
He stated we could. And almost simultaneously we agreed, one or
both of us, that it would be a good idea to put the water on either side
of 6221 to prevent any spread of the flames. And that was in the time
frame of approximately ten of or five of, when we first knew that there
was fire on the roof. I was still desirous of removing the bunker . . .
There was no way that I could order him. I sincerely hoped for his con-
currence.

Thus was the decision made to use the fire on the roof in a tactical manner. Later on it became clear that the fire was no longer containable, or
as the fire fighters say, "incipient." Sambor was asked if he tried to find
out why the water was not on: "A. Not particularly sir . . . Because it
was not my job. Q. Whose was it? A. The Fire Department's."[37]
Sometimes collaboration between equals is the key frame. Sometimes it is clear-cut division of labor. Sometimes it is situational hierarchy. Orders clearly take on a phenomenological life of their own. It
would be too reductive to say that what we have here are participants
simply passing the buck. Ethnomethodologists have taught us that
something truly complicated lies in the negotiation of shared agree-
ments. And theorists of bureaucracy have taught us that such complications ensue even in an organizational framework that has tried to
eliminate the negotiations necessary to taking action.

The Fragmented Bureaucratic Self: Bringing Emotion Back In

We have already heard a suggestion of sentiment in Richmond's and
Sambor's references to desire. Richmond talked of the possible desire of
the police commissioner that the fire fighters shut the hoses down.
Sambor told of his desire to remove the bunker. This is a strange word to
find cohabiting with orders (although perhaps no stranger than *insinuations*). It is joined by diverse references to emotions by all of the Big
Four.
Bureaucrats not only do not need emotions to do their job, they must
excise their emotions to do it. Beyond the epistemological problems
with this, as outlined by Gerald E. Frug and others, is the problem of
communicating the nature of decisions and decision making to a public
that resists accepting the complete split between public and private in
their political leaders and other public officials. Parenthetically, they
also resist being forced to split themselves when dealing with these offi-

cials. The public looks for some seamless blending of public and private, of objectivity and emotion, from their leaders and want these leaders to view the public, as so composed. Yet what we find instead is a situation in which both leaders and public are forced into a state of "doing emotion." This is structurally identical to the operation of "doing being ordinary" discussed in chapter 3, which focused on the public as represented by the neighbors of MOVE. Here the doing of emotion makes the expression and reading of emotion anything but seamless. It often seems as if emotion is imported into or superimposed on the bureaucratic persona. The stitches between bureaucrat as impersonal, machinelike, efficient and bureaucrat as human being with feelings are glaringly apparent. Let me provide some telling examples.

On the day of May 13, Mayor Goode was caught between a tactical police plan already in action and some community negotiators who came to his office to try a last-ditch effort. He tried to describe his position of bureaucratic fatalism to the MOVE commission by attempting to embrace and bring together all of the personae that inhabit his being. "But for my own point of view . . . once we had made the decision to make those arrests, . . . some form of armed confrontation was inevitable . . . And I tried everything that I knew how as a person, as a Mayor, as a human being, as a parent, to avoid this but, I did not see any way it could, in fact, in the long run or in the end, be avoided, I should say."[38] Goode did indeed distinguish among these roles or personae. And here he tried to cobble them together, to make the "parent" join forces with the "mayor." But these fragments of a self do not come together to give an image of a three-dimensional, coherent being. They remain separate, like beads on a necklace, now one, now another brought to bear on a complicated and wearing situation. In fact, the distinctions he made seem like absurd splittings of hair. What is the difference between a person and a human being, for example? The bureaucratic self in crisis has fragmented beyond even organizational logic.

At a point in the questioning of each of the Big Four witnesses, MOVE commission members asked a question specifically about emotions. They essentially asked the witnesses to do emotion. Goode was asked what, if any, emotions he went through as he saw the fire rage on his television screen. He replied: "I went through very deep emotions at that time. I cried because I knew at that point that lives would be lost . . . And I can't explain to you or to anyone the kind of emotions that I went through because everything about me is about preserving life and to know that any plan that I've had anything to do with would, in fact, bring about the cessation of life was very tough."[39] The emotions were deep, but they cannot be named, and they were only explicitly acknowledged when essentially coerced by the questioner.

Regardless of its sincerity (not an issue here) or its psychological pathology (also not an issue here), how convincing was Goode's doing of emotion? Not very, according to some community residents interviewed in the American Friends Service Committee study. A Ms. T recalled: "When [Goode] said, 'I did it, and I'll do it again,' something inside me just turned 180 degrees in the opposite direction . . . I said, 'He's under a lot of pressure' . . . but nothing would make you say that. And there was no feeling of remorse. I saw no expression on his face."[40]

Goode is not the only one whose emotion work appears odd or out of sync. Managing Director Brooks made similarly strange references to his emotions. "Q. . . . but did you have any realistic expectation that in fact [MOVE members] would come out upon a mere verbal request? A. Then I probably—I had an emotion that they might come out or that those who wanted to come out might come out."[41] Brooks referred to an emotion as if emotions were a kind of bacterium, something one has in spite of "realistic expectations," something that comes from the outside and inhabits one's being uncomfortably. Fire Commissioner Richmond also had an emotion scene in which he broke down while recounting his participation in a ceremony to remember fallen fire fighters soon after the MOVE confrontation. "Q. Would you like to take a short break? A. No. I will fight through it. The two reasons were: One, the four kids out at MOVE . . . And to know that they died by fire, I will have to live with that. But on the other hand, I broke down because there were no new names of police officers or firefighters added . . . I know what happened, but I am emotional about it."[42] Emotions have their moments, brief and intense. But they must be summarily brought into the discourse and ejected or "fought through" quickly. If emotions were sustained, if the person and the parent and the mayor converged, if they were part of "realistic expectations," the bureaucratic discourse of instrumental rationality would crumble under the weight.

From the other side of the official divide, the neighbors and former MOVE members who came into contact with the city administration encountered similar discursive constraints and symbolic contaminations of the sentimental into the bureaucratic and the bureaucratic into the sentimental. Louise James, testifying in front of the MOVE commission, began her opening statement by starting that "it is not easy for me to be here; not easy for me to try to keep a tight rein on tense emotions that are at best fragile." But quickly afterward she asserts: "I am objective. Because I am objective, even though I realize that this is the Mayor's hand-picked panel, it is only fair that I not assess you until there is something to assess."[43] Emotions are no replacement for objectivity as a legitimate ground for participation in an official, inquisitional setting.

Finally, how do we understand, going back to the issues of control and of discursive interaction, the strange scheduling of Mayor Goode's meetings with the distraught neighbors, the scheduling of the neighbors' meeting with MOVE, MOVE's scheduling of its first loudspeaker harangue, and the scheduling of the May 13 operation? All of these occurred on holidays except for the final confrontation, which was specifically rescheduled to avoid a holiday. The loudspeaker harangue began on Christmas Eve 1983. MOVE members and the neighbors met on Mother's Day in May 1984. The neighbors and the mayor met on Memorial Day 1984 and on July 4, 1984. Finally, the serving of arrest warrants, originally planned for Mother's Day 1985, was postponed by one day. Can this holiday mania be a coincidence? Or does it signify something about the way the problems that plagued the Osage Avenue block were viewed? Were they viewed as marginal, slotted into the corners of the calendar? Or, not really in opposition to the last notion, were holiday meetings analogous to Marie-Antoinette's dictum, "Let them eat cake!"? Were they supposed to draw all of the participant's attention to the sentimental, the domestic, attention that was perhaps, in the case of MOVE's decision about the timing of the loudspeaker, sometimes ironic, but for the other participants "sincere"? Perhaps the final images juxtaposing and combining the bureaucratic and the sentimental should be two that concerned the prospect of finding the former Osage Avenue residents new homes after the fire destroyed the block. Thomas Muldoon, president of the Philadelphia Visitors and Convention Bureau, referred to plans to rebuild the homes: "And if they're in by Christmas, I can't think of a better date."[44] At the same time, Mayor Goode was quoted as saying that "the city law department's special claims unit would investigate the damage, promising the agency will go around and make sure that those persons who feel they have in fact been damaged in any way can file their claims appropriately."[45] The appropriate filing of forms and the gifts of Santa Claus are forced into an uneasy and delirious cohabitation.

CHAPTER FIVE

The Law and Its Apparatus
Speaking Warrants and Weapons

In social life this [satisfaction that others have met with a just punishment] occurs in general wherever antipathetic people or members of an unpopular minority put themselves in the wrong. Their punishment does not as a rule correspond to their wrong-doing but to their wrong-doing plus the ill-feeling directed against them which has previously been without consequences.

Sigmund Freud, *The Interpretation of Dreams*

When a person breaches the law, his moral character is transformed in the eyes of society. Adherence to the law is regarded as so vital that an effort to evade its judgement in a large number of cases is sufficient reason for a person's exclusion from that community, and even his legal execution. Policemen kill people for crimes that would earn them only small jail sentences, but nobody seems to view this as a situation worthy of remedy.

Jonathan Rubinstein, *City Police*

Armed confrontations like that of May 13 seem to erupt with a sudden ferocity. But clearly, there is a legal and judicial context out of which the arrest warrants, the police, the antitank guns, and the explosives emerge. They do not leap, fully armed and armored, like Athena from Zeus's forehead. In this chapter I trace the contours of that context, charting its development as the situation on Osage Avenue was defined and redefined in the legal and military idioms of the authorities ultimately responsible for determining the shape of the confrontation. I elaborate the phenomena and phenomenology of such things as warrants and entry devices/bombs. And I analytically tie these two kinds of objects together. Ultimately, I am concerned with the relationships between legal language, decisions, and documents and the police, force, and violence.

In the highly specialized occupational structure in which we live, we tend to think of occupations as insulated worlds. They have purviews and discourses completely intelligible or meaningful only to those who operate inside them. Calling such worldviews "disciplines," Foucault tried in his later writings to catch the threads of the different disciplines of knowledge and power and to show how they were all caught up in the circulation of power in modern society. There are, at particular moments of disciplinary interchange, moments when one discipline hands off a charge to another discipline—here the moment when lawyers hand warrants to police. What must transpire to bring such moments into being and what happens after such moments occur? How are the transferred objects and ideas interpreted by subsequently responsible disciplines?

Several writers have interrogated the specific territory where legal deliberation and physical pain are linked. Kafka and J.M. Coetzee are two novelists who have illuminated the connection. Among scholars, Elaine Scarry has explored the notion of "legal confessions" in the context of torture. And Robert Cover strips law of its disembodied pretenses: "The relationship between legal interpretation and the infliction of pain remains operative even in the most routine of legal acts . . . [But] I do not wish us to pretend that we talk our prisoners into jail. The 'interpretations' or 'conversations' that are the preconditions for violent incarceration are themselves implements of violence . . . The stay of execution . . . shows the violence of the warden and executioner to be linked to the judge's deliberative act of understanding."[1]

In the MOVE case the specter of violence was always present. Those responsible for policy and for legal processing were well aware of their own participation in the violence of the state, that last resort and first premise, recalling Weber, of the state's existence. But they represented their violence-activating actions as having been willed by a force greater than themselves, something almost like fate. So many officials expressed a sense that a violent confrontation between MOVE and the police was inexorable that it made their own legal and deliberative actions seem almost superfluous. One has to read the process of the evolution of the actual arrest warrants very carefully to identify choices, moments of decision making that mattered. One also has to look hard to find alternative choices posed by those in touch with the legal departments of the city, but with different discourses and different mandates.

Clearly, what goes on in the decision to codify, approve, and serve arrest warrants is more than what the prosecutor in the Ramona Africa conspiracy and assault trial made it out to be when he said: "What it really comes down to is a police officer with a warrant attempted to serve that warrant at a person's house. All he's doing is trying to serve an arrest warrant and somebody in there is trying to kill him."[2]

The Language of the Law

According to Richard Ericson and Clifford Shearing, there are two distinct faces of the law, one symbolic, the other operational. Legal discourse must appeal to values and principles to provide specific laws and, simultaneously, their merits. It must also move along the terrain of coercion, control, and force. Resistance to and transgressions of the law are a given. Someone has to do the dirty work. "There is the discourse of the public culture: its normative sentiments about the rule of law provide a legitimating symbolic canopy for the work of police and other legal agents. There is also the discourse of the operational reality of social control on behalf of the state: the law allows police and other legal agents to take the actions they deem necessary, and yet be able to construe them and account for them in terms which make them publicly acceptable."[3]

The law exists as a codified, if evolving, set of constitutional provisions and amendments, legislative statutes, executive orders, judicial opinions, and criminal codes. Yet there is no easy one-to-one correspondence between the occurrence of an action, the determination that that action constitutes the specific breaking of a law, and the decision to arrest the actor for that transgression. Layers upon layers of intervening discretion, knowledge, compromises, and interpretations break apart the theoretical correspondence. These intervening considerations often come as a surprise to a trusting or naïve citizenry. As one neighbor of MOVE, Clifford Bond, noted in his opening statement to the MOVE commissioners: "The word 'law.' A system of rules formed to protect society. That's a real joke. The laws were not applicable, I was told, and I would still like somebody to explain to me why not."[4]

What Is a Crime?

At various points during the long history of the MOVE/city/neighborhood conflict, diverse institutions and individuals had to decide whether one or another behavior of MOVE members constituted a crime. Many of these protagonists found themselves operating in a nether world of codes and ordinances, norms and mores, parole violations and suspicion of terrorism. Such a world is engulfed in a kind of miasma in which context and discretion provide the only answers to the question, What do we do? In these contextuated decision-making processes, several overriding criteria dominated. One criterion was the professed (by the mayor and the managing director) concern about civil rights violations if MOVE members were arrested. Another was the specter of violence that hung over the fortified MOVE house if even a License and Inspection employee attempted an inspection. Still another was the uncertainty of individual police officers about how to categorize the behavior they would witness—which rules applied. Asked to explain his behavior toward MOVE during the year before May 13, Civil Affairs Division officer Theodore Vaughn stated: "If there was a crime being committed by a MOVE person in my presence, I would put them under arrest. Other than that, anything else that was not a felony would be considered—to take the information down and turn it over to the DA's office to find out if criminal charges would be placed . . . Misdemeanor, harassment or something like that . . . I would have to be told what Criminal Code it came under so that I would be aware of it. I don't know every misdemeanor crime that's committed."[5]

There are an honesty and a looseness in Vaughn's statement. It is a looseness that citizens such as Clifford Bond find an irritation and a betrayal. But what Vaughn is attesting to is the constructive and interpretive power of those charged with social control to define situations. He simply brings to life the analysis of Ericson and Shearing when they state: "The police officer sifts among the rules as they can be used to normatively construe the facts, thereby translating the matter before him into an acceptable account and ultimately transforming it into something which meets established criteria of rational acceptability."[6]

The problem with MOVE, however, was that no one seemed to be able to work this situation into one of "rational acceptability," and the agents of the state kept batting the facts around without settling on a definition. Specific charges had been levied against individual MOVE members. Frank Africa was wanted on a parole violation. Ramona Africa was charged with failure to appear in court for a disorderly conduct hearing. But as Frank Rossi, columnist for the *Philadelphia Inquirer* asked, "Are these crimes worth dying for? . . . They are so far out of the mainstream of our society that people wanted them out. And what about the cops? What officer wants to die arresting people for simple assault and health-code violations?"[7]

This discrepancy, an overt disparity between an assessment of the lower-order magnitude of the crimes and the calculated physical risks in any interaction between MOVE members and police, is a mirror image of another discrepancy in this case. This discrepancy is the strange coupling of the willed ignorance of those "in charge" on May 13 of the actual contents of the arrest warrants and their willingness to bring the most extraordinary arsenal to the scene.

None of the Big Four knew what the specific charges against certain of the MOVE members were. Not even Sambor, who read the "Attention MOVE" statement to the house on Osage Avenue, read the arrest warrants. This ignorance, both casual and conscious, signified a kind of leap of faith for those in charge, faith that their chosen means fit the crimes and the people charged. We can call it faith, instinct, or a discursive blank spot; at whatever level of analysis it was wildly excessive. Certain crimes do tend to be associated with set levels of police force. When one simply doesn't know what crime one is dealing with, the level of force has no logical parameters.

If there was a general but unnamed or variously named presumption of MOVE criminality on the part of those in official position, such a presumption was also shared, ironically, by members of MOVE itself. Yet here the register was different, both sarcastic and fearful. MOVE members knew that they could always be arrested for *something*. On the day of May 13 itself, last-minute efforts to talk MOVE members out of their house were being frantically, if haphazardly, made. One Civil Affairs Division officer, James Shanahan, was in indirect contact with a MOVE member who did not live on Osage, Jerry Africa, about his possible appearance. The intermediary was an organic mediator, Judge Robert Williams; Williams finally had to report to Shanahan that Jerry Africa was not going to come. Shanahan testifies about this revelation: "I said, 'What's the matter?' He said, 'He's afraid . . . you're going . . . I don't know whether he was afraid—afraid or afraid he was going to be arrested or both . . . And I said, 'Well, what is he going to be arrested for? We don't have anything to arrest him for.' He said, 'He thinks you're going to arrest him.'"[8]

Who Can Be Guilty?

This discussion must not only address the crimes alleged to have precipitated and warranted the operation of May 13, but also those that were alleged to have emerged precisely from that operation. Eleven people are dead, and 250 people are homeless. Can notions of blame and guilt be used? Are they appropriate? In order to answer these questions, we must ask, How do our legal doctrines frame guilt?

For my purposes, the most significant thing about the process of locating guilt is that only individuals can be found guilty. While it is true that corporations may be fined for wrongdoings such as polluting the air, and so forth, only individual employees of such corporations can go to jail. Worldviews, institutional processes, and governing structures cannot be indicted. As John MacAloon writes: "It is an essential feature of North American constitutions that the state cannot itself be brought to trial. In return for guaranteeing citizens equal rights before the law, the state as an entity is given immunity."[9] In the MOVE case two grand juries were not able find any specific individuals who could be held directly and criminally responsible for these deaths and displacements, and no one was indicted. We have seen in our analysis of the self-representations of actions taken by those "in charge" that they felt themselves and the situation to be "out of control." They were "diligent," "desirous," and "concerned," but they were not in control. Thus a fine line is discursively constructed between negligence and malice, and that line provides immunity. It is hard for us to even imagine an alternative, practical language of guilt that identifies and indicts structural or procedural guilt rather than individual guilt. While theorists such as Hannah Arendt have tried to develop a theoretical language for talking about the guilt of bureaucratic rule, for example, the practical translation of such a language often reduces the indictment to individual terms.

Even those participants in social conflicts who are anti- or extra-institutional ultimately engage a discourse of individual guilt when casting blame. In her statement on the final report of the Philadelphia County Special Investigating Grand Jury, Ramona Africa noted that "what really makes us so bitter is that nine innocent MOVE people are in prison for 100 years each for a murder that nobody saw em commit, a murder that nobody can prove they committed, cause they did not commit it. At the same time, the whole world saw system officials drop that bomb on us, killing eleven innocent MOVE people and these officials is still walkin the street, still employed by this system, and still bein payed with the tax dollars to keep on murderin money-poor, unofficial poor folks."[10] And prodded by a question from the MOVE commission staff ("In your opening statement, you said that you witnessed murder. Could you tell me who it is that you consider to be a murderer?"), Novella Williams, organic mediator, responded: "Whoever carried out, whoever made a decision to drop, to use high powered weapons on people in my community . . . whomever ordered that a bomb be dropped; whomever allowed the fire to burn while I watched helpless, when no one would listen, while big chunks of debris was falling on me, are murderers and they must pay."[11] These unnamed, but theoretically nameable, individuals remain immune, however, enveloped in their institutional structures and prerogatives.

Even with this presupposition of individual rather than institutional guilt, and with the virtual immunity of individuals institutionally grounded, some gaps remain. Given the magnitude of the destruction and death of the operation of May 13, the normal process of granting immunity to legitimate authorities doing their legitimate jobs (force and all) fragments inside its discursive constraints. This is most clear in the categorizing decisions of the various medical examiners who had to determine the causes of death of the eleven people in the MOVE house. The Philadelphia Medical Examiner's Office classified all the deaths as accidental. Ali Hameli, a forensic pathologist and an expert witness brought onto the case by the MOVE commission, disagreed. He divided the deaths between the MOVE children, which he classified as homicide, and the MOVE adults, which, while excluding accident, he could not classify; "Is it suicide? Is it homicide? I cannot determine that." Even more significant, in the case of the apparently clear determination of the manner of the children's deaths, he actually managed to indict a process as the culprit—the *interactions* among various adults (including officials, MOVE adults, and police). Thus for those responsible for naming death, the discursive limitations of the legal categories were obvious and stymying. Guilt, in this case, ends up being located everywhere and nowhere at the same time.

Speech and Crime

An issue of the law that was salient in this case is the relationship among speech, rights, and crimes. The fact that MOVE members mounted a loudspeaker on the outside walls of their house and harangued neighbors through that loudspeaker with language viewed as profane and threatening lay at the heart of the conflict between MOVE, neighbors on Osage Avenue, and the city officials. According to an April 1985 police information report, this broadcast speech included the following: "We are going to put Mayor Goode in his mother——g grave." (Note that the word *fucking* is never spelled out in the police report.) "We are going to put bullets in his head." "We are going to blow his motherf——g head off." "We are gong to City Hall and take his motherf——g life." "Wilson Goode don't deserve to live." "We have 12 years of bullets for his head." "We are going to kill any motherf——g cop that comes to front, back or on our god dammed [*sic*] roof."[12] Other police surveillance reports and tape recordings made by the neighbors on Osage Avenue dating back to 1984 revealed similar threats and statements being made about President Ronald Reagan. How was this speech heard and categorized? Given the extant laws on speech how might it have been categorized?

In the summer of 1984 Managing Director Brooks attended a meeting at the local FBI office to discuss the contents of the loudspeaker harangues. He recalled that meeting during the MOVE commission hearings: "After more and more pronouncements of intent to do bodily harm and then the adding of the President of the United States to that, the Mayor felt that it was time that we sat down with all of the people involved. Because when you include the President, it then becomes a Secret Service matter . . . the meeting concluded in a rather obscure way, that none of the Federal agencies thought that there was anything that they should do about it, that they could do about it . . . but to just watch it some more."[13] Several things seemed to be involved in this decision. One was the asserted preoccupation with violating MOVE's civil rights, a preoccupation that was discursively plied throughout the talk of legal authorities in this case. One must assume here that the reference was to MOVE's right to free speech. But how could an overt, public threat to put a bullet in an elected official's head be construed as falling within the purview of the First Amendment? Certainly, in the early 1990s debates rage over whether hate speech is protected by the First Amendment. But one might think the case is clear if an outright threat against the life of the president is made. Yet even this is more complicated than appears at first blush. According to Danet, Hoffman, and Kermish, there are competing interpretations of the relevant law, Statute 18 U.S.C. 871(a)(1970), originally passed in 1917. They identify the "objective" and the "subjective" interpretations:

> The objective interpretation of 871(a), that there need be no proof that a defendant intended to carry out his or her threat or entertained any bad purpose in making his or her statement is supported by one reading of the legislative history of the statute . . . [Justice Marshall proposed instead] that 'the statute should be construed to proscribe all threats that the speaker intends to be interpreted as expressions of an intent to kill or injure the President . . . the majority of cases has followed an interpretation of the statute in which the prosecution must prove that any reasonable person hearing the utterance in the context

in which it was uttered would arrive at the conclusion that this was a serious threat.[14]

What was the reading of the threats made by MOVE? Perhaps the lack of federal interest derived, paradoxically, from their familiarity with MOVE, the knowledge that MOVE had consistently made such threats and never followed through with them. Perhaps the federal agents were anticipating a subjective reading to the statute, assuming that the threats were part of "just a strategy," as Jerry Africa once claimed, and not meant to be interpreted as serious.

Of course, for the neighbors the loudspeaker speech continued to be a vexing presence, upsetting them with its "character assassinations" and disturbing their children with its inescapable profanity. This speech had a paradoxical nature, at once public in the sense that it was broadcast and available to anyone in the area and private in the sense that it insinuated itself into people's homes. It could not be avoided or turned off. Again, working with our common-sense notions of public and private, it was public in that it was broadly about the oppressiveness of the "system" and private in that it delved into the intimate, if often imaginary, details of the lives of specific individuals. For the officials the speech was a categorical mine field—slander, political speech, bona fide threats, and so forth. And while it opened up the terrain for interpretation, it ended up closing down the terrain for action.

The Genesis of an Arrest Warrant

In this section I trace the trajectory of a legal process whereby actions and interactions in a neighborhood are translated into documentary evidence that in turn is translated into an arrest warrant. That nothing is fixed or automatic about the relationship between a given crime and a given legal response should not, by now, surprise. But the degree to which interpretive work on the part of those with the power to act dominated the MOVE case is noteworthy.

Although many city agencies and offices were involved over the several years of the MOVE conflict, in the end it came down to the actions and decisions of the mayor and the district attorney's office. These two institutional locales were ultimately responsible for taking legal action against MOVE. It was not until the early summer of 1984, however, that the mayor asked for a focused review of and memo about the MOVE members on Osage Avenue. Edward Rendell, then district attorney, recalled that review of the evidence to see if there were sufficient grounds for arresting one or several MOVE members:

> I asked Bradford Richman [assistant district attorney] and people from our Law Division . . . to sit down with the police and go over what evidence that they accumulated . . . the review consisted mostly of going over police reports and documents that the police had prepared, the Police Intelligence reports. I don't think at the time we talked to any civilian witnesses. I think we went over a great deal of both written reports from police, tape recordings and photographs . . . I asked them to . . . one, set forth what they believed the evidence indicated in light of the prevailing sections of the Pennsylvania Crime Code; and two, the strategic—and I mean strategic from the standpoint of legally strategic pluses and minuses of various courses of action. I don't mean strategic in terms of physical assault.[15]

There are two very interesting aspects of this rendition of the process engaged by the district attorney's office. First, the "evidence" consists, in one sense, of an arbitrary and delimited set of objects. Ever since the ethnomethodologists did their studies of the social construction of such things as data and records, it has been impossible to accept any formal document as naturally corresponding to some uninterpreted or un-worked-on object in the real world.[16] The work of institutions in processing their objects of concern involves the creation of categories, the conventionalizing of procedures of description, the delimitation of relevant data, and so forth. In the case of the district attorney's office, a set of institutionally constructed items that included certain things (police reports and documents, tape recordings of the bullhorn, and police photographs) and excluded others ("civilian" witness reports) was calibrated against another constructed object, the Pennsylvania Crime Code. Thus the evidence was summoned at a certain moment of time, a moment that announced its significance as MOVE members threatened to demonstrate in commemoration and persisting anger over the anniversary of the August 1978 Powelton Village MOVE-city confrontation. The peremptory summoning of the evidence crystallizes that documentation in the files of the police and the district attorney and withdraws it temporarily from the complex historical and institutional context in which it is but a part.

The second interesting aspect of the district attorney's statement is his use of the word *strategy* and his immediate insistence that he is using the term in a very proscribed way. He is most careful to distinguish legal strategy from anything having to do with "physical assault." The oblique reference here is obviously to the police, whose strategy is inevitably involved with force and violence. Thus in direct contrast with the connection Robert Cover draws between the actions of lawyers, judges, bailiffs, and so forth and the actions of police, wardens, and executioners, Rendell is explicitly severing that link by claiming only a strategy of legal "courses of action." Further, given the extremity of the force used by the police in the May 13 operation, Rendell may also be marking that gap between the handing off of an arrest warrant and the actual serving of it.

Despite the summer 1984 memo forwarded to the mayor, no action was taken until May 1985. What was involved in the decision not to act? Those in the district attorney's office referred to two factors, a certain institutional psychology cultivated by a generalized atmosphere of reluctance (recall the FBI's admonishment to attend to the issue of MOVE's civil rights) and a sense of a broader context. Both an assistant district attorney and District Attorney Rendell spoke in peculiar and revealing terms of this period after the writing of the memo. Assistant district attorney Eric Henson spoke of being in touch with the Parole Department to see if they wished to proceed with the parole violation warrant against Frank Africa in the summer of 1984. He described this process of various legal departments feeling each other out and summarized: "I think that gives the history of our subjunctive mood . . . with regard to the warrant." Similarly, Rendell spoke of the fact that the "memo did not ripen into arrest warrants" at that time.[17] Both a "subjunctive mood" and a process of "ripening" suggest a world in which decisions are not obvious, in which possible worlds open themselves up despite crime codes, legal statutes, and uniformed police. An arrest warrant can be stillborn, an institution of the state can slip out of a declarative mood and into a subjunctive one.

Mayor Goode identified the context as having been responsible for the unripe arrest warrants of 1984: "The decision that we had to make . . . was whether or not to go about and confront the MOVE house over 1 or 2 warrants and . . . what they [the district attorney's office] regard as misdemeanors . . . that to go in and to make the arrest of one or two people would in fact possibly provide them with that platform [of publicity] and would do nothing, nothing whatsoever to cure the problems that the neighbors were in fact concerned about."[18] This is a strange admission by Goode. This reasoning imagines weak warrants (that are not linked to major offenses and will only provide publicity for the enemy and strong warrants (unacknowledged but implied) that would be matched with egregious crimes, perhaps federal offenses, and would most likely engage and/or elicit violent action in their serving. We find here a kind of structural analogue to the slogan of some European terrorist groups of the late 1970s, out to push the system to implosion: "The worse, the better." Only the worst crimes on the part of MOVE could solve the problem.

One party seems to have been significantly excluded from the warrant preparation process, the neighbors, or "civilians," as the district attorney named them. In the several years in which MOVE members lived on Osage Avenue, the neighbors contacted and wrote to many elected officials and a myriad of city agencies and offices (including License and Inspection, Welfare Department, Commission on Human Relations, managing director's office, mayor's office, police department, Streets Department, Highway Department, and Health Department) about their problems with MOVE. Yet they did not even make it into the category of evidence, as determined by the district attorney's office. This exclusion says much about the notions of witness or victim held by the officials in charge. As we shall see in dealing with the role of the organic mediators, the notion of *witness* particularly was whittled down and made passive. A civilian witness at most might be a recording machine but more likely was simply employed as a voice that confirmed an already scripted official story. It was only in the spring of 1985 that the neighbors even entered the evidence ledger in an official capacity. And that entrance, many believed, was precipitated only by a press conference that the neighbors held, in which they finally threatened to "take things into their own hands." Autonomous action could be prevented only by official inclusion, and thus on the last Sunday in April 1985, twenty residents of Osage Avenue were driven to the district attorney's office to be interviewed and to provide affidavits against MOVE. This last-minute and peremptory inclusion was not satisfying to those whose voices were being solicited. Here is how one neighbor describes her interview.

> I—I'm a respectable person of those in authority. And in fact, Rendell's office, under false pretense to me—we were under the impression that we were going to meet with him himself, not underlings or someone who was assigned at the last minute to come and take statements from us. And they were hours or so picking us up . . . They wanted information within the last 90 or 120 days that had gone on on the block . . . And when I told him about the gasoline [on the roof], he told me I didn't know what I was talking about, that I was making an

assumption . . . And the whole time he took the statement he was very arrogant. And like it was a bother to him to be there on this Sunday.[19]

The absent forms of social respect were clearly salient for this participant/witness: punctuality, politeness, and the sense that one is viewed as credible and important. Further, for the purposes of codifying arrest warrants, the entire history of MOVE's relations with the other residents of Osage Avenue was to be telescoped into the "last 90 or 120 days." Finally, a crucial piece of information, the existence of a gasoline can on the roof, was dismissed as an "assumption," something that this witness, restricted in terms of the interpretative action she was granted, was not entitled to make. Entrance into the realm of evidence was thus highly conditioned, the organizational procedures of data creation in full force.

Representations of the institutional will, or "mood," varied during early May 1985. The *Philadelphia Inquirer* retrospectively described the Big Four as having "decided collectively to forcibly evict MOVE, if necessary. In order to commence their operation, the Police Department needed legal justification to enter the house and remove the occupants—either arrest warrants, a search warrant or both."[20] Here the impulse for action is portrayed as flowing in a different direction—the police want to move and thus must have some legal basis for so doing. Does this reversal of the flow of initiating action matter? Or does it simply appeal more to our cultural sense of civilian control over the paramilitary forces in our society, to believe that the process is actually a loop from commitment of crime to reporting of crime to calibration of crime to police operation? This division of legal labor, calling forth interpretations and actions from several agencies and forces in no single prescribed sequence, raises a question about the evolution of the process of approving warrants in general. Martin Grayson, writing on the history of the search warrant, notes that "general warrants were issued only to private persons or companies . . . [this is] significant because it raises the question of whether the drafters of the 4th Amendment anticipated our vast network of policemen, district attorneys, sheriffs, marshals, legislative investigators and Drug Enforcement, Treasury and FBI agents."[21]

Finally, after so much time, so many memos, letters, and meetings, it all came down to a few days of concentrated official activity. Arrest and search warrants that included charges of terroristic threats, harassment, threats and other improper influence in official and political matters, criminal conspiracy, possession of explosives or incendiary materials or devices, disorderly conduct, and riot were finally approved at a meeting on Thursday, May 7, and signed by a common pleas judge on Saturday, May 11, for the arrest of four of the MOVE adults in the Osage Avenue house. Of the May 7 meeting Edward Rendell said: "I have attended a lot of meetings since I have been in public life, but I never ever had attended a meeting that had the impact on me that my meeting on Thursday, May 7, 1985 did, when in fact the plan of action was signed, sealed and delivered; when the arrest warrants and the search warrants were approved, [to be] signed by a judge: when we had picked a time and date to act; when we knew it was going to occur. There was almost a dread in that room so thick you could have cut it with a knife."[22]

Negotiation in the Interstices

What then of the possibilities for a negotiated settlement of the MOVE/city/neighborhood conflict? How might the "operation" have been alternatively configured? Various representatives of such community-oriented city agencies as the Crisis Intervention Network had been told that MOVE was now a "police matter" and that their participation was no longer required. What happened to the discourses of negotiation as the dominant discourse of battle got set in place?

All disputing comes to life through language, as Conley and O'Barr attest: "Early in our study we were drawn to the conclusion that at any particular point in time the dispute is the account being given at that time."[23] And the physiognomies of disputes change in conjunction with changes in their discursive framings. Disputes may begin as a conflict between two parties. As third parties and official agents of legitimate authority get drawn into the orbit of a dispute, the discourse of the dispute shifts accordingly. Mather and Yngvesson have elaborated what they call a continuum of discourses of disrupting, "with everyday discourse at one end and a highly specialized 'language of the law' at the other."[24] Here I am interested in that mode of talking disputes that may lie somewhere in the middle of the continuum. This may involve official city negotiators, with a mandate and a somewhat specialized language (perhaps including a bureaucratic language of *clients, rights,* and *neutrality*). It may also involve more informally trained community activists and advocates whose language is perhaps more complicated and less predictable. Negotiation, then, turns out to engage a possible mix of discourses—the formulaic and the hybrid. In the MOVE case, there were both.

Who Were the Potential Negotiators?

Those people running official community-oriented city agencies prevaricated somewhat on their own sense of their respective mandates and powers. Even before the phrase "a police matter" locked into place, the only approaches to the MOVE conflict were diffuse and episodic negotiation/dispute resolution. John White, Sr., director of the Community Intervention Program, claimed that he had neither the expertise nor the resources to deal with MOVE and had characterized the conflict as "too hot to handle."[25] Bennie Swans of the Crisis Intervention Network asserted that "we have no direct responsibility for interaction in situations such as MOVE . . . the commitment or involvement really derives from our staff's association, affiliation and commitment within the neighborhoods in which they live."[26] And Gloria Sutton, of the Philadelphia Commission on Human Relations, found her mediation efforts rebuffed by the neighbors of MOVE on Osage Avenue because "the residents of Osage decided they did not want a mediator, they wanted an advocate. They believed their personal attempts to settle their differences with MOVE were mediation enough."[27] The sense of responsibility and efficacy of these city agents was, then, highly qualified. Some felt out of their depth, some based any involvement more on personal community history and knowledge than on official mandate. Others were discouraged by the alternative framing articulated by the neighbors. Rather than being the clear emissaries of official civilian power, these fragmented agents tried, but could not find, their own authoritative discourse.

Extramural negotiators, or organic mediators, also actively if belatedly pursued a peaceful resolution to the conflict. The term I use, *organic mediator*, derives from Antonio Gramsci's notion of organic intellectuals, who are not other-class imports into a community (in Gramsci's work, a working-class community) but rather are internally elaborated. In other words, they are their community's own intellectuals (or activist/negotiators in this case) and can move back and forth physically and discursively across the borders of the community. Called "citizen negotiators" in the MOVE commission report's list of witnesses, these individuals were all members of the wider West Philadelphia community. Their testimony at the MOVE hearings positioned them as being able to communicate across several lines of social differentiation. They did not officially represent the City of Philadelphia, MOVE, or the neighbors of MOVE in the period of their activity, right before the confrontation. They defined themselves as self-activating with clear, though bounded and intermittent, authority.

The self-constructions of the organic mediators are extremely significant, particularly in light of the alternative ways those in positions of authority construed them and their actions. They were generally marginalized and ignored by those in charge of the operation of May 13. Mayor Goode, for example, spoke in a causal and uninformed manner about one group of organic mediators active on May 13, 1985. Goode described this group in a press conference that day as "a group of clergymen and heads of organizations and members of varied groups around the city who have been active in things like this across the years. I don't know their names. I did not take their names."[28] This is a discourse of accident—things happen, groups flow into and out of the conflict. There is that same persistent representation of authority and situations out of control. An enforced sense of anonymity and looseness is associated with the group of would-be negotiators whose precise organizational and issue affiliations are consigned to the phrase "active in things like this across the years." Of negotiation in general, Police Commissioner Sambor's assessment was that "negotiations have constantly failed with the MOVE personnel, and if it became necessary after the evening when we fell back and regrouped and started again the next day, then that use of hostage negotiations may well have been the tactic that we used. But it was not a tactic or consideration at that time."[29] Here what impresses is the military language used to construct all participants and actions, from MOVE "personnel" to hostage negotiations as a "tactic." Given these official attitudes, it is not hard to understand organic mediator Novella Williams's experience at the police barricades on Osage Avenue on May 13: "They were ignoring you. No one would listen. I saw—now that I know his name is Captain Shanahan, and I tried to identify myself to him. I even went as far as to tell him that I had worked with Inspector Fencl during other crises of this nature and he just brushed me off. He later came to me after the incident and said he just didn't know who I was. What a shame. But I never got a chance to really talk to anyone because they were ignoring me."[30]

The organic mediators make only a brief and shadowy appearance in the final report of the MOVE commission (another authority in its way, though significantly after the fact). The relevant passage reads: "Formal and informal city groups chartered to deal with these kinds of problems were rebuffed and discouraged by the Administration from mediating or otherwise offering their services. Into this vacuum stepped a number of community mediators with no active mandate from the city administration" (p. 24). Here, the organic mediators are distinguished from any "true" (if underused) negotiators, those who lay claim to the legitimate authority of the city. The organic mediators are positioned in this text merely to signal the city's incompetence, not, as might be the case, their own suppressed competence.

Negotiation Grounds

In the process of identifying specific issues that might be amenable to negotiation, the potential negotiators were attempting to tell the story of MOVE and its conflicts in precise and diverse ways. Mather and Yngvesson describe two opposing processes of classification of disputes, narrowing and expansion, that act to set the parameters of say- and do-ability as regards any particular conflict: "Narrowing is the process through which established categories for classifying events and relationships are imposed on an event or series of events, defining the subject matter of a dispute in ways which make it amenable to conventional management procedures . . . Expansion, in contrast, refers to rephrasing in terms of a framework not previously accepted by the third party . . . challenges established categories for classifying events and relationships by linking subjects or issues that are typically separated."[31] Some of the proposals put forward on or prior to May 13 acted to narrow the dispute; others attempted expansion. Of course, we must keep in mind the significant fact that none was successful.

According to the *Philadelphia Inquirer,* in the period immediately prior to the May 13 operation, three semiofficial negotiators (including the husband of Mayor Goode's chief of staff) were in communication with members of MOVE and brought to Goode the demand that there be no immediate arrests upon MOVE's potentially relinquishing its Osage Avenue home. On the Friday before the serving of arrest warrants, Goode was quoted as saying that indeed there would be no immediate arrests, although he wasn't promising anything about the future.[32] These demands sound like a surrender on MOVE's part and at the same time have the ring of "terrorist-type" demands: an outlaw group wants a safe getaway. These quasi-negotiations acted to narrow the classifying categories by accepting the MOVE-as-terrorist definition. Regardless of Goode's sincerity or ability to make good on his word on that Friday, there is a decontextuated and unreal quality to this interchange.

Going back some time in the past, we find a very different notion of negotiation put forward originally by Bennie Swans, head of the Crisis Intervention Network. In a June 18, 1984, letter to Mayor Goode (interestingly coincident in time with the district attorney's memo to Goode), Swans wrote: "In order to buy time, I recommend that some discussion take place around the use and time of the loudspeaker system. While clearly negotiating around the speaker system will not serve as a resolution, it does provide more time. This may minimize chances of a forced reaction by the law enforcement community and may allow for the development of a more creative approach to handling the MOVE organization."[33] Mayor Goode did not take Swans up on this suggestion, and nothing more was said of it. It is, however, an analytically interesting angle. Swans is here immersed in detail; one might say he ignores the forest for the trees. Certainly the loudspeaker was a key issue for those living on the block, but it was one of many that made up the MOVE problem. What were the assumptions of Swans's suggestion? First, Swans is implying some sort of possibility of dialogue with MOVE members, implying their responsibility. He also asserts an acceptance (however temporary and strategic) of the presence on the block of MOVE and its loudspeaker. This negotiating position is very contextuated and comes from one who clearly knows the situation well. MOVE is not reduced here to terrorists. The times and spaces of the neighborhood lives and life-styles are at issue, and both sides would be required to alter some assumptions about what occurs in these times and spaces. Obviously, it is impossible to know if such a negotiating strategy would have worked, bought time (as Swans framed it), or failed.

Finally, given the intermittent but persistent identification of MOVE members as terrorists by city officials, it is somewhat startling to discover a posited negotiation position on their part that seemed extremely orthodox and conservative in its terms. I refer here to the desire of MOVE members to have a judicial or executive review of the 1978 incident–related charges for which the nine incarcerated MOVE members were serving time. Asked by the MOVE commission to relate a conversation he had with Conrad Africa some time prior to May 13, Bennie Swans revealed Conrad's proposal. "Q. Did Conrad Africa tell you what it would take short of an actual confrontation or a concluded compromise to make them turn down or cease their activities which were so affecting the neighbors? A. Conrad alluded to a process . . . something that would begin to investigate, something that we begin to review the charges of conspiracy that they felt were trumped up against their members, that that would be sufficient to break the impasse."[34] Indeed, on the Friday before May 13, Robert Williams, an organic mediator, did meet with Jerry Africa to discuss the possibility of gathering a group of lawyers to review these charges.

A "review of charges" has such a benign ring to it. It seems quite the opposite of a terrorist incident of exit and escape from a hideout. It also opposes itself to an alternative image of MOVE that derives from attending to the language and the referents of the language of the loudspeaker—the wild threats (including the unconsciously rather comic one of tying up all of the traffic in Europe, along with the threats against the lives of the mayor and the president), the profanity, the character assassinations. Finally, it opposes itself to the characterization of MOVE by some organic mediators who in the past had claimed that MOVE could not "articulate their needs in such a way that other people can understand it. If this is not done, there can't be any resolution."[35] Once again, we find both a chasm and an overload in the realm of interpretation of What is MOVE? And once again, the only "found" resolution was annihilation.

The Establishment of Credentials: The Case of the Organic Mediators

Of the various organic mediators who came forward on and around the period of May 13, three were called as witnesses during the MOVE commission hearings. (It is interesting to note that out of the thirty-six sessions in all, the organic mediators were called for one session, various members of the Philadelphia police force for nineteen.) In their testimony they established their mediating/negotiating credentials, their own discourse of experience and competence. The discursive strategies employed by incumbents of official positions, including the members of the MOVE commission, repositioned these individuals as accidental witnesses to a tragic event. In exploring these discourses, I bear in mind Peter Goodrich's analysis of the theoretical personages available for legal discourse: "The semantic preconditions of legal discourse, the legal world view, may be summarized in terms of procedures of individualization and generalization—both narrative and justificatory—which work to manipulate and transpose existent human beings and groups—the diffuse, complex and changing biographical and social entities of motivated interaction—into the ethical and political—rhetorical—subjects of legal rationality and formal justice."[36]

Novella Williams, fifty-seven years old, founder of Citizens for Progress, a civic group in Philadelphia, said in her opening statement:

I am indeed happy to have this opportunity to share with you some of the things that happened on that tragic Mother's Day weekend, May 1985. I believe I was a witness to murder . . . I have lived with my husband and our children for more that a quarter of a century within 10 blocks from the scene of the Mother's Day tragedy. I see no reason to leave my area now. I have stood up with my community when my people were threatened. I'm recognized for my willingness to respond and take effective action and I will do no less here today . . . People in all walks of life know what I'm about; Heads of State, municipalities and officials and city departments, educational institutions and just plain old ordinary people like me . . . I was there in the mean streets of this nation, Selma, Montgomery, Washington, Mississippi . . . Check the record, it's all there . . . I stood on the steps of 6221 Osage Avenue, Sunday May 12th, Mother's Day. I talked to Theresa Brooks Africa, while helicopters circled over the rooftop . . . I saw how frightened the children appeared to be . . . This was an unbelievable force against so few men, women and children . . . Yes, I believe I was a witness to murder. I tried to save their lives and their houses. I talked, I watched, I cried and I prayed that somebody would listen . . . We the government are not allowed to kill our people because they dare look different, behave obnoxiously, have a different lifestyle or disagree with the system.[37]

In Williams's statement, she positions herself as a specific kind of participant and witness, a watchful, active, experienced, and evaluative witness. In the moments of textual repetition she overtly calls attention to the power of this role, particularly the repetition of the line, "I was a witness to murder." In this phrase, she names herself as present, she gives herself a title—witness—and she does not hesitate to name the crime. Further, in the course of the entire opening statement, she constructs her own autobiography by referring to previous occasions of community and civil rights conflicts and by naming her actions: "I have stood up," "I responded along with many others," "I was on the front lines," "I am called upon," "my demonstrations and negotiations." The autobiographical authority constructed here is based on her presence at specific sites of conflict, her experiences there, and recognition by an assortment of public and private constituencies. My concern is not with the actual extent of this witness's reputation. Rather, it is important to note that the autobiographical authority being established in this discourse is not constructed via a listing of affiliations with official organizations or a listing of degrees in specific training programs, school, or, significantly, branches of the military.

Charles Burrus, another of the three organic mediators called to this session of the MOVE hearings, stated that he had "fallen into a role, more or less, of negotiator . . . Me not being that familiar with the legal system, I don't know if I'm using the proper terminology. Fortunately, in my life style, I was able to stay out of the [legal system] . . . We were acting as mediators instead of negotiators . . . No one asked me to negotiate, I negotiated on my own, as a concerned black man."[38] Burrus, like Williams, declines a self-identity of official expertise. In fact, he asserts a certain fortunate ignorance of the law and legal language. He claims an autonomous initiative based on a notion of responsibility to those of his own race, and it is the term *concerned* that provides the grounding for his authority.

Given these alternative discourses of authority voiced by the organic mediators, how were they received by those in positions of legitimate, formal authority? We have already heard Williams declare her frustration at not being listened to by the police at the scene. And we have heard Mayor Goode dismiss their efforts with a casual reference to a group of individuals whose names he had not learned. I now turn to the way the MOVE commissioners construed these individuals as witnesses, in order to examine more closely the discursive process of disaccreditation.

Immediately following Novella Williams's opening statement, the commission's deputy counsel says to her: "I will return to you in a moment and we'll ask you some questions specifically about what you saw and heard on the days surrounding May 13th." This may appear an innocuous and obvious response of counsel, but it directly repositions the witness away from an active, engaged participant and toward a passive recording machine. Counsel is only interested in getting information about what Williams "saw and heard," not about what she thought or did. Counsel is interested only in details. Thus many questions are about the clothing worn by the MOVE members with whom the mediators spoke on the day of the confrontation. Were the MOVE children in shorts and tops? What color were the tops? Did the men on the roof have beards? How much, approximately, did the woman on the steps in front of the house weigh? These questions had their motives. The bodies recovered from the MOVE house were in such bad condition that identification was not certain. But the organic mediators disclaim their "expertise" as recording machines. Williams states that she was not thinking about what they were wearing. "I was just looking at the person." Charles Burrus, when asked about the children's clothing says, "My state of mind at that point was to save human life and I was committed to go back and forth as many times as I could to do that and really didn't pay any attention to things like clothing even though it's very important now."[39]

The organic mediators pose themselves as active interpreters, social agents with power. They are not reluctant to move across domains, even those about which, as in Burrus's case, they claim a certain ignorance. They operate in their neighborhoods and in the realms of official authority. And their discourse is a complicated hybrid of the concrete and the analytic. Listen to interchange between Burrus and one MOVE commissioner, a lawyer and former Pennsylvania State Supreme Court judge. Burrus is asked:

> In your conversation with any of the people to whom you spoke [among whom were MOVE members not living in the Osage Avenue house] did they ever state a demand other than they wanted the convicted MOVE members arising out of the 1978 incident out of jail? A. Your Honor . . . I don't think that, you know, my interpretation— what was relayed to me is the concern wasn't just to bring those people out of jail. The concern was to have someone in the judicial system to hear the hearings. Q. Well, was the Mayor told that there was any demand other than the people getting out of jail that would get the children and the people out of that house? That really is my question. A. I understand your question again . . . So not to be debative with you but to say that [Jerry Africa] asked me to say—to get his people out of jail—that he never said that to me direct and what he kept stressing to me, . . . the three-hour conversation was we want to begin the process so that our people—their hearing—they can be heard. And like I said, I'm a novice to the judicial system, so I don't know the proper terminology.[40]

The distinction is subtle but important—release MOVE members unconditionally or start a judicial review—and the witness presses the subtlety. One more example reveals an "organic" discourse conscious of its own flexible metamorphoses. Novella Williams recounts a phone conversation she had with Mayor Goode on the day before the confrontation: "I asked the Mayor as humbly as I could, I even called him His Excellency, if he would please reconsider the action that was about to take place. I told him that there were children in the house . . . I thought maybe if we could continue talking we might be able to accomplish a peaceful end or at least save their lives, because I told the Mayor that I was convinced that if there was a police assault on that house that the people would be killed. Q. And what did the Mayor say? A. He told me that he had been assured by the experts that no one would be hurt."[41]

Here Williams underlines her own discursive strategy of humility in talking with the mayor. She pays deference by calling the mayor "excellency." But she self-consciously highlights her deference by calling attention to it precisely as a narrative strategy. She also does not hesitate to assert her own reading of the possibilities of violence and death. In this case, humble certainty is met with the certainty of one who puts faith in experts. Perhaps the organic mediators provide us with an example of a split subjectivity, paying deference, speaking humbly, but certain of a different vision. Mary Louise Pratt presents and elaborates on the theory of class language practices and split subjectivity put forward by Noelle Moreau: "Moreau argues that 'each class speaks itself according to the same hidden referent. This social referent is the dominant group . . . [B]ecause the social referent is the same for all classes, class language practices are not homogeneous and this non-homogeneity is necessary for language domination.' Dominated groups, in her view, are forced into what she calls a split subjectivity, because they are required simultaneously to identify with the dominant group and to dissociate themselves from it."[42] Perhaps, as we saw in the case of the sentimental discourse in chapter 3, such a split subjectivity is a discursive knife that can slice both ways.

A final example of differing notions of knowledge, witnessing, and involvement involves a tangle between a former MOVE member (the mother of one of the MOVE members who died in the fire) and the MOVE commission counsel. Very early in the MOVE hearings two of the first witnesses, Louise James and Laverne Sims, are being questioned by the main MOVE commission counsel, William P. Lytton. Lytton is referring to the day of May 13, 1985, when these two former MOVE members had ostensibly been given the opportunity to communicate with those in the MOVE house through a bullhorn. James and Sims, her sister, had apparently declined that involvement, citing the difficulty of negotiating anything "standing on a corner." Lytton's next question is, "Did you or Mrs. James have a concern at the time that you had the option of speaking to the people inside that house that the people in that side [sic] of that house might be in physical danger or that lives might be in danger?" Following is much of James's response.

Ms. James: Concern? We knew it.

Mr. Lytton: Mrs.—

Ms. James: Excuse me. You had two hundred boot-kicking Gestapo-oriented cops out there that day. You had that day a police officer by the name of Mulvihill who was in the 1978 tragedy, who was in fact one of the officers who stomped and kicked and beat and bludgeoned and shot and helmeted and kicked some more my brother, Delbert Africa . . . Yes they were professionals. Professional boot kickers, professional murderers, professional rib crashers, professional head busters, professional back stabbing cops, professional killers . . . But the point that I'm trying to make is that the day that Delbert was beat, when those cops beat that boy so bad, they were being observed without knowing they were being observed. When we saw Delbert . . . His ribs, every one of them were broken. His face looked like chopped liver. He was limping. He could hardly walk . . . I said, "My God, Del." And Laverne and I broke down and we cried, and Delbert broke down and he cried. That man was in so much agony from that beating. And you turned right around on the 13th of May and you sent this same mentality Mulvihill out there to do the very same thing. And you ask us to believe in you legal—your justice. There is none.

BY MR. LYTTON:

Q. So as I understand your testimony you were concerned that there may be physical harm to the people inside that house; is that correct?

A. I believe, Mr. Lytton, that you are insane.

Q. My question is—

A. Excuse me.

Q. Yes, ma'am.

A. I heard the question. Would you turn up your hearing aid, please? . . .

Q. Yes, ma'am. Do you have something to say?

A. You asked me that in the beginning. I have just gone through an entire litany—

Q. I know.

A. —of what happened on August 8 of 1978. I have explained to you. I don't talk in hieroglyphics here. I speak perfectly good English, and you understood it. For you to sit there and listen to what I have just said and come back and ask me were we concerned is complete insanity.

Q. My question is: Is it only for political reasons that you decided not to take, even if it was a small chance, the opportunity to try and get those children and the people out of the house when it was offered to you?[43]

This extraordinary exchange provides a glimpse into the political dynamics of testimony in formal hearings when the parties are of unequal social status and when the subordinate party is conscious of and unwilling to accept the dominant party's frame. On the surface, Lytton's question seems straightforward enough: Did the former MOVE member have a concern that the current MOVE members were in danger on May 13? But it is quite clear that the question is so obvious that it is either purely procedural, reducing James's and Sim's witnessing modalities to a simple rehearsal of the obvious, or the question has an ironic trapdoor of logic (if you had concern, why didn't you try and talk them out) waiting at the other end of the response. But James does a rather extraordinary thing with this question. She shoots out the other side by immediately demonstrating, with the long and gruesome litany of the injuries suffered by MOVE members in the past, the insufficiency of the term *concern*. And then, after Lytton essentially repeats his question, implying that it had not been adequately answered by her historical narrative, James pushes aside the boundaries of even the looser inquisitional interrogation frames and questions first Lytton's sanity, then his hearing, and finally his very cognitive and linguistic abilities.

Clearly, James's mode of doing "being a witness" is much more aggressive and reactive than is normal. She goes so far as to problematize the legitimacy of the interrogator, on a number of grounds. She speaks a language of emotion and experience, something she shares with the organic mediators. But perhaps what is most interesting about this exchange is that James uses her language of experience to explain her *lack* of involvement on May 13. Just as now she problematizes the boundaries of witnessing, so did she problematize the opportunity for "involvement" given her by the police on May 13, 1985, by refusing the bullhorn.

Final Arbiters of the Law: The Police

In the months and weeks before May 13, the Philadelphia police were handed control over the MOVE crisis by several city and federal agencies. Mayor Goode declared MOVE "a police matter" and instructed Commissioner Sambor to develop a plan; Managing Director Brooks told community-oriented agencies they were no longer involved; the district attorney set the grounds for arrest warrants, to be served by the police; and the federal law-enforcement agencies said they did not believe they should be involved. With the various civilian mediators, official and unofficial, marginalized, the police were the court of last resort.

The Dialectics of Police Presence

Even in the best of circumstances, the presence of police raises "civilian" anxiety and preoccupation. Recently, the Pennsylvania State Troopers Association called my home to solicit a holiday donation, and the caller began his pitch by saying, "Don't worry, this isn't anything official, it's just a courtesy call." Wielders of official violence, bearers of writs of regulation and social control, the police are aware of their own charged presence. Of course, the valence of citizen response will vary, according to times of day, place of encounter, neighborhood experience with the police, and other demographic factors of group membership. Harvey Sacks writes: "There are places where the police can count on the presence of two of their cars to provide for their visible, legitimate presence, such that others will then search the scene to find what the police might be doing that they should be doing . . . Whereas there are others who . . . seeing two police cars on the scene may now look to see what kind of bother the police, by being on the scene, are producing as compared to what kind of bother they are properly responding to."[44]

Police operate on a border between the world of legitimate activity and the world of crime. They must move back and forth between these two realms, their asserted goal to prevent contamination of the former by the latter and to vanquish, or at least suppress, the latter. But the police must themselves traffic in the land of the contaminated, with the very weapons of the contaminated. They constantly reveal the violence of the state in their uniformed appearance and their methods. Scholars who have studied this ambiguous identity of the police have drawn attention to such things as moral relativism found within police forces as violence is deployed in quasi-legal ways (Gary Marx and John Van Maanen), to the ambivalence evoked by being a declared regulator of people's conduct (Jonathan Rubinstein), to demonstrating the remnant of the archiac forms of violence in contemporary civilized society (Peter Manning). While such ambiguities and doubled identities seem analytically obvious and largely unavoidable, they often strike the public as intolerable. Speaking about Mayor Goode's perceived lapse in his ability to control the Philadelphia police, a citizen surveyed in the American Friends Service Committee study said: "It's the responsibility of a Black elected official, who has responsibility over the police force, to ask the questions that whites don't ask, and to make certain that the . . . Commissioner of Police doesn't simply manifest . . . a police mentality."[45] That the police manifest a police mentality makes sense in the world of abstract theories of the division of the labor of social control in society. On the streets of a real city, with all of its tensions of race and class, it can come to seem a dangerous proposition.

What are the contours of a "police mentality"? What are the structures and themes of police organization? Daniel Swett writes that "the police . . . are more than a group of individuals organized into a bureaucratic, paramilitary structure to perform technical missions. Entry requirements, training, on- and off-duty behavioral standards, and operational exigencies and goals combine to produce a homogeneity of attitudes, values, and life ways such that members of police forces constitute a distinct subculture within their societies."[46] Among the features of this subculture are loyalty to each other, particularly to one's partner, and, according to Swett, a classificatory schema that perceives the culturally different as threatening.

Like all other police forces in northeastern cities in the United States in the 1980s, that of Philadelphia confronted a city in which basic production jobs, the jobs of unskilled and semiskilled labor, were in sharp decline. Poverty, crime, drugs—all of the charged terms of modern urban life were as salient here as elsewhere. But the Philadelphia Police Department had a particular character that was reflected in the way it was deployed in the MOVE operation.[47]

The police department was still slowly pulling itself out from under the weight of the Frank Rizzo legacy of brute force and hostility toward racial minorities. The department was under federal investigation during the period of the early and mid-1980s. As Jack Nagel writes: "The Federal investigations . . . were not only for corruption, but for the brutality and civil rights violations."[48] The quality of the recruits was also at issue, with unclear entrance-test standards and no minimum educational degree required for admission. In terms of general orientation, Jack Greene (personal communication) noted that Commissioner Sambor tended to emphasize the weapons and tactics side of the force (given his history in the organization and his continuous membership in the National Reserves) rather than the community relations side. This tendency was apparent in Sambor's selection of planners for the May 13 operation. Finally, there had been a long legal struggle to integrate the force. William Brown III, lawyer and chairman of the MOVE commission, had written in the 1985 Urban League report that "the Philadelphia Police Department, for example, has been the target of equal employment litigation. The increased number of black police officers in Philadelphia is a direct result of that litigation. Now that the Philadelphia Police Department has increased its number of blacks and other minorities, the department is a much more sensitive organization and is, indeed, more responsive to the legitimate concerns of the black community."[49] Others, including a former FBI agent and chief investigator for the MOVE commission, derided the minority hiring practices of the department, claiming that "they have never made any progress except that which was required of them by the courts . . . Once again, attitudes have not changed at all."[50]

Police Language: Public and Private

It was nothing for us to be walking down the street and . . . on occasions where police would ride up and make obscene gestures to us, call us niggers, talk about our hair.

Larry Howard, MOVE supporter

Studies of medical students and doctors at work have revealed some nasty ways that these professionals talk in private with each other about their patients. Sociological analyses have interpreted such moments of black humor as tension releasing, a way to deal with the pressures and the tragedies of hospital life. Similarly, it is clear from ethnographic studies as well as from the various leaked audio recordings of police radio communication that police engage in a private, and no so private, language of racial epithets and profanity to talk about their "clients." (The recent case of the beating of Rodney King has brought this practice into high relief.) I'm not sure that one of these subcultural forms of private trashing of the public should be considered justifiable and one considered heinous, just as I am not sure they are completely structurally analogous. In any case, these matters might be considered trivial but for two relevant issues. The first issue is free speech versus hate speech. To what degree might a police officer's reference to a person as a "nigger" constitute a civil rights offense? To what degree might a police car radio be considered a private arena, to what degree public? To what degree does such a racist term signify or create an image of the individual that provokes unequal treatment? The second issue is the role of language in general in the entire MOVE conflict. We have looked in great detail at the ways in which the language of MOVE members was heard and represented by a variety of parties—neighbors, city administrators, and police. The threats of assassination were clearly one point of contention, but interestingly enough, the persistent use of profanity grated even more on the law-enforcers in all official arenas. Generally, in memos, in newspaper interviews, and in the publicly broadcast MOVE hearings, the police would not say or write the word *fucking* when recounting the MOVE member's language. This public prudishness puts the private language in a different light.

Jonathan Rubinstein, in his wide-ranging and detailed ethnography of the Philadelphia Police Department in the late 1960s and early 1970s, links language use to issues of power. "Nor is physical force the only way a policeman may violate a person. He can take an insulting tone, talk down to someone, adopt a familiarity that is unwanted but cannot be stopped."[51] Rubinstein notes that police have a license not only to be violent in our society but also to be rude, an unusual combination of freedoms. But where, given the constitutional issues of free speech and civil rights, does rudeness bleed into oppression? One chief of police encountered by Jerome Skolnick in his study *Justice without Trial* actually issued a form of "oppressive speech" directive to his officers that sought to control these derisive terms and, at the same time, ironically gave evidence of their pervasiveness and prolific generativity.

> As a matter of policy, the following words and any other similar derogatory words shall not be used by members and employees in the course of their official duties or at any other time as to bring the Westville Police department into disrepute. These words are: Boy, spade, jig, nigger, blue, smoke, coon, spook, headhunter, jungle-bunny, boogie, stud, burrhead, cat, black boy, black, shine, ape, spick, mau-mau. The most common display of a lack of courtesy or objectivity is the use by an officer of unsuitable or offensive language or mannerisms. There is a particular need to refrain from language which has a derogatory connotation with reference to race, color, religion or nationality. Such usage by the police causes deep resentments and antagonism against them.[52]

This directive is interesting in a variety of ways. The main issue at the time of its writing (1960s) is the possibility of these terms' evoking antagonism against the police, not the possibility of abusing someone's civil rights. Further, the chief first seems to say that it is only in the course of official duties that police must watch their words, but then he adds "or at any other time." I think there is real confusion about when police are on- or offstage, and this is reflected in the directive. The line between the two is quite thin, and particularly in the case of police controversies offstage behavior and speech become the focus of public scrutiny. This is exacerbated by the increasing reliance of police forces on technological means of communication, record keeping, and information gathering. In such cases the technology is, for the police, a knife that can slice both ways. Before exploring the implications of such technological windows, let me say that only one police officer in the MOVE hearings voluntarily and spontaneously recounted the utterance of profanity, his own use rather than MOVE's. This officer used it in his narrative only when describing his conversation with Ramona Africa during the moment of greatest danger and chaos on May 13, that moment when Ramona emerged from the burning house and the officer ran with her to the waiting police vans: "I said to her, 'Is any fuckin body else in the house?'—Sorry everyone.—She never answered me."[53] Note the instant apology. Even in extremis, the use of profanity still represents transgression.

The Phenomenology of Police Violence

It is an uncomfortable commonplace that the police employ violence in the course of their work. Somehow, given our civilization's rhetorical queasiness about circulating agents of violence, the police must translate its use into publicly acceptable terms. Even the term *social control* seems quiet and orderly, despite its Kafkaesque tone. Some official statements about police behavior that is viewed as excessively violent, such as the 1968 Violence Commission report, engage in a discursive reframing that mutes the actual phenomenon by calling it something else. Elliot Currie writes: "The Report never uses the term 'violence' when discussing the behavior of police and other officials . . . In several places the Report is regretful of the use of 'excessive force' by police, but it does not mention police 'violence.'"[54] This is noteworthy in a report that, even in its title, is centrally preoccupied by violence.

   In the MOVE conflict the police were the agents of last resort for a city and a neighborhood that could or would not find other means of resolution. They were called in as saviors of the neighborhood at the very moment, interestingly enough, that the neighbors of MOVE threatened to transmute themselves into vigilantes. But what did these saviors do? They displaced the neighbors by evacuating the block. They insinuated themselves into the neighbors' homes, hoping to gain access to the MOVE house. They blew up the homes with explosives, creating internal holes through which to launch tear gas into the MOVE house, and they watched these homes burn down. They shot high-powered weapons at a house in which there were children. They killed, or were catalysts of the deaths of, eleven people. How did the police translate this degree of death and destruction into a public language that asserts the legitimacy of the police to engage in violence on behalf of society?

The key issue is the notion of limits. The police have the discursive burden to assert that the violence of the operation corresponded to specific parameters of necessity—the means matched the ends. The police oscillated between two discursive poles in the accomplishment of this task. Sometimes they invoked a language of war, implying that the overwhelming arsenal brought to bear on the MOVE house matched the scale of the conflict. Sometimes they invoked the language of the domestic sphere, mostly the kitchen, implying that the relevant arsenal was a relatively tame and benign collection of items. Thus they alternately raised and lowered the volume by deploying diametrically opposed discourses to describe the same event.

Several interrelated types of limitations do or should theoretically constrain the actions of police. First, there are the limits of time. Although police are granted the authority to use violence whenever they believe it is warranted, they are formally constrained by such things as a sense of the contextuated danger to self or others and by constitutional constraints on violent means when other means are available. Still, although police are often called upon to justify the use of violence after the fact, Peter Manning writes that "its use cannot be predicted by law or police regulations."[55] Thus the unpredictability of police violence must somehow be considered, despite the limits articulated above, part of the very structure of the police role itself.

The next analytical limit regards the extent and type of police violence. As we have seen, the Big Four's ignorance of the exact nature of the crimes identified in the MOVE arrest warrants preempted any sense of proportionality of tactics to crimes. This kind of phenomenological context for force includes such things as the nature of the crimes, the anticipated response of the accused, the individual policies of a given police department, and the available technology and weaponry.

The final limit corresponds to the definition of the situation. This is obviously linked to the specific nature of the crimes, and so forth, but goes beyond that to name the broader context. Perhaps here the notion of a continuum of situations eliciting force is useful, with Wall Street junk-bond dealers at one end, escorted peacefully (although always with the background threat of force) into their minimum-security jails, and a type of criminal "war" at the other end. Violence is extremely limited at one end of this continuum and extremely extensive at the other. As Jonathan Rubinstein writes: "Only when martial law is decreed is the policeman authorized to exercise force without limitation and these measures are generally accompanied by the introduction of soldiers, whose training and equipment prepare them to control people by brute force."[56]

The Technology of Excess

A few years ago, while on a speaking engagement at the University of Toronto, I happened to stumble into the annual meeting of the International Association of the Chiefs of Police. The convention was huge and seemed focused mainly on a giant hall of exhibits. Bright lights, sound-track narrations, glossy posters—all advertised a literal explosion of technology available to the modern law officer. There were fancy lights for patrol cars, high-powered rifles for the marksmen, devices to gain entry into locked areas, something obscure called "the jaws of life," surveillance equipment, and even a robot that kept assaulting the conventioneers. Technology and weaponry clearly dominated, and the one small booth set up for community relations seemed dull and shabby by comparison. This convention, taking place just two years after the MOVE confrontation in Philadelphia, was clearly invested in a technological approach to policing. In this regard, the prophecy of the Kerner commission report of 1968 was born out: "The Commission condemns moves to equip police departments with mass destruction weapons, such as automatic rifles, machine guns and tanks. Weapons which are designed to destroy, not to control, have no place in densely populated urban communities."[57]

What were the weapons and other equipment that were brought to Osage Avenue on May 13, 1985, by the police? There were tear gas (whether merely "harmful" or "fatal" is questionable, as we shall see), various explosives (Tovex and C-4) to blow holes in the sides of the MOVE house, smoke bombs and other camouflaging devices to allow for police entry into the houses bordering the MOVE house, and a variety of guns, rifles, and antitank weapons. Sergeant Albert Revel, asked during the hearings to recall the logic of equipment allocation, stated: "From the best of my recollection, what I heard was that the Commissioner wanted to know what we had in our armory as to the availability of automatic weapons. And he was told we have, you know, that all the

16's and the UZI's and the 50's and . . . Lt. Powell said at the time that he had the availability of getting some other heavy automatic weapons and he wanted the advice of the Commissioner, whether he thought it was necessary for them to get them. Q. What did the Commissioner say? A. He said, 'If you can get them and they can be transferred legally,' he says, 'get them.'"[58]

There is a sense here of a largely indiscriminate process of gathering weapons together that have no specific relationship to a prescribed and delimited plan. It is bricolagelike in style; anything that the policeman has available to him (within the thin limits of legality) can be used. This approach to weapons was matched by a similar approach to personnel; anyone who was available in the designated units of the police, regardless of past experience with MOVE, was called to the scene. Further, there was a singularly bricolagelike improvisation of weapons. Some stun grenades, for example, were homemade by the Bomb Disposal Unit when professionally made ones were unavailable.

Participants in the MOVE confrontation were called upon before, during, and after the event to describe, catalog, and justify the use of specific kinds of tear gas, explosives, and guns. It was clear to all that something dreadful had happened. The smoking remains of two city blocks and the removal of bodies remained indelible. How could the "tools" of this operation be articulated? One discursive idiom voiced a strangely folksy narrative of police rooting about in the pots and pans of a generic kitchen-arsenal to devise tame and familiar "entry devices." For example, Goode slid around a bit in his version of this idiom as he conflated the terms of potential devastation: "Q. Was there any discussion on May 9 . . . about the children in the house and the effect of tear gas on the children? A. I was told that [the police] felt that the tear gas being used would not, in fact, be fatal to the children. Q. Would not be what sir? A. Fatal. Q. How about harmful? A. Harmful, fatal, I use the words as the same."[59]

Tear gas was indeed used, and Goode, for all his strange conflations, was reflecting a pervasive ambiguity about the exact nature of this tear gas. Commissioner Sambor claimed the "less debilitating" kind of tear gas (CS) was used, but he was referred to a MOVE commission document that indicates the "more debilitating" type (CN) was actually used. But testifying officers did not engage an idiom of (more or less) debilitation when asked to describe their weapons. For example, a series of questions put to high-level police officers testifying at the MOVE hearings, about how to characterize one type of powdered tear gas, elicited analogies to talcum powder and salt and, finally, from one chief inspector, the following: "The closest I can come sir is powdered milk."[60]

Domestic items pile up, as in a delicatessen. Tovex explosives are described as a "salami" and a "hot sausage." A Federal fogger is said to sound like a lawn mower. Charges placed on internal walls of the houses next door to MOVE are described as looking like a "kid's platform for trains." We have here a mirror image of the self-presentation of the neighbors, who similarly deployed icons of the domestic sphere. There is clearly a cultural power in the act of discursively appropriating the kitchen and the backyard, and the only thing that might surprise is the variety of situated agents engaging in it.

The various explosives used during the day of May 13—the salamis, the train platforms, and so forth—can be said to have culminated in the satchel of explosives dropped from a helicopter onto the roof of the MOVE house in the early hours of the evening. This first-ever experience of the Philadelphia police force in the use of explosives for tactical purposes may strike us as strangely reminiscent of the book *Fahrenheit 451*. For the (misnamed in this case) Bomb Disposal Unit put this explosive device/entry device/bomb together and arranged its "delivery." Testifying police officers and city officials of all ranks consistently referred to this thing as a *device,* with the variations of *entry device* and *explosive device* coming and going. Such a discursive framing performs a service for those intimately associated with destruction. Carol Cohn writes of this service: " 'Clean bombs' may provide the perfect metaphor for the language of defense analysts and arms controllers. This language has enormous destructive power, but without emotional fallout . . . these words may also serve to domesticate, to tame the wild and uncontrollable forces of nuclear destruction."[61]

Thus did state trooper and helicopter pilot Richard Reed claim that he didn't wonder about the people inside the MOVE house because he understood that the thing being dropped out of his helicopter was an "entry device." Thus did Managing Director Brooks deny that what was dropped was a bomb, because "my connotation of a bomb is a device designed to destroy. A device designed to—usually in a steel casing, usually with some kind of fins on it to direct it or some kind of propulsion to guide it. And in that connotation it was not a bomb. If in the connotation that it's falling from the air makes it a bomb, then in that connotation it was a bomb."[62]

Of course, if the only things that were being hurled at the MOVE house on May 13 were salamis and powdered milk, it still left the ques-

tion of how so much actual destruction came about. Some police officers, when confronted later with photographs of the blown-off fronts of
the houses contiguous to the MOVE house, expressed surprise at the
amount of damage caused by "low-order explosives." The testimony
and media interviews of other police intermittently engaged a discourse
that varied from that of domesticated weapons. And this was the discourse of war. It somewhat ironically relied upon the assumption that,
as one officer put it, "I believed [MOVE members] were as well equipped
as we were." In reality, only five weapons were found in the rubble of
the MOVE house on May 14. These included one Mossberg shotgun,
one Remington .22 rifle, one 12-gauge shotgun, one revolver, and one
Charter Arms .38 Special revolver. None were automatic weapons.

Videotape and Terror

Two police officers from the audiovisual unit of the police department
were assigned the task of taking photographs and videos of the May 13
operation. The photographs revealed a gap between the alleged low-
power explosives used and the high-power destruction evident as they
documented the demolition of the front porches of adjacent houses. The
short bit of video tape revealed a similar problem. The segment, shown
several times during the MOVE hearings, acted as a kind of ritual repetition, demonstrating over and over, both for those witnesses being asked
to comment on, interpret, or implicitly apologize for the clip and for the
watching public, the potential for psychological and moral abandonment at the heart of all "legitimate" violence. The segment follows a
few minutes of tape taken from a police post across the street from the
burning MOVE house. The tape shows the inside frame of a second-
story window and through it, the burning house. Voices are heard in the
background, some distinct, some laughing, and one clearly saying, "I
guess they're never going to call the Commissioner a motherfucker
again." The scene shocks in its brutality and its casualness. A fire burns
out of control, no water is being sprayed onto it. Eleven people are somewhere inside, and MOVE's language is still for the police the singularly
preeminent transgression. Here in the tactical post of battle, it is interesting to note, the police do not hesitate to say the offending word.

The use of videocameras by police, bystanders (Rodney King's beating), and criminals (a Queens, New York, teenager taped a friend mug-
ging another teenager in November 1991) represents a qualitative
change in the capacity of social agents to expose private experience to
public scrutiny and, alternatively, to protect private infractions from

public evaluation. Although several testifying police officers were asked to identify the speaker of that line about the commissioner, none did. In a sense, it is simultaneously the voice of none of them particularly and all of them generally. In the MOVE case, many of the elements of the MOVE-city conflict are concentrated in this one brief taped scene—the offensiveness of MOVE's language, the schizophrenia of police language, the excessive violence of the police, the anarchy at the heart of the city's approach to MOVE, and the actual abandonment of the rhetorical idols (MOVE children). No wonder the tape was played over and over in an almost obsessive search for moral understanding.

One strand of the military discourse carried a considerable share of the burden of that search. That strand involved the claim that MOVE members were terrorists, a term that, in 1985, seemed to have been imported from an international context of hijackings and knee-cappings.

Just before the break in the afternoon session of October 23 of the hearings, commissioners asked the following question of a witness, Police Captain Edward McLaughlin:

> Q. I'm concerned in the future about trigger words and we've heard witnesses talk about terrorist groups and Commissioners talk about terrorist groups and I guess I'm concerned in the future that somehow if something is labeled as terrorist, a separate group of rules will apply. Is there now any definition in the Intelligence group of the Police Department or anywhere within the Philadelphia Police Department? . . . What is a terrorist group? Is there a formal definition? A. I think we accept the fact that we use the same definition as everybody else in the world does. . . . I think if you listen to those people who have lived on that street for years . . . I don't recall we have any directive specifically on terrorists.[63]

Both the assertions and the admissions in this exchange about terrorism echo through the various sessions of the hearings, as the commissioners attempt to lasso together the term *terrorism* and its empirical referent. The goal might seem modest and obvious. But achievement proves elusive. While the term *terrorism* is promiscuously deployed to refer to the MOVE group throughout the hearings (recall Commissioner Sambor's assertion that MOVE was a terrorist group), the "definition" of it is never fixed. Captain McLaughlin repeats what other witnesses say in so many words, "we use the same definition as everybody else in the world does." That definition, however, cannot be spoken. While there may indeed be strategic reasons for those engaged in the practices of law enforcement and policy-making to shy away from the constraining business of definition mongering, such shunning suggests something more profound.

The use of the term *terrorism* to capture the reality of MOVE exaggerates and exposes all of the usually suppressed anxiety associated with the word. The label *terrorism* acts as a bridge connecting an imaginary world inhabited completely by a violence without reason with another imaginary world inhabited totally by language and void of violence. Disorder, irrationality, unpredictability—a human wilderness on the one side. Order, reason, predictability, domesticity on the other. The term announces the attempted incursion of disorderly and unpredictable violence into the calm world of the "normals." But the power of the term lies in its ability to both mark and deny this connection of the two worlds at the same time. Its categorical claim is that their connection is transient, accidental, and external—the worlds are mutually exclusive. The term is equally effective in denying that the connection is internal—that domesticity can beget terror or that disorder has its reason. The term exists to cite the connection, but in its inability to define the set of its referents, the *terrorism* label also performs the denial. Beyond the label, no extended discourse can illuminate the meaning of the term. The two imaginary worlds float conveniently apart, again upholding the acclaimed mutual exclusivity of violence and language.

Terrorism is thus explicitly opposed to legitimate violence. Some might claim that the phrase *legitimate violence* is simply engaged to justify attacks against those transgressing social boundaries. While not refuting the viability of this claim, I believe the case is much more complicated. In the MOVE hearings the city officials, MOVE commissioners, fire fighters, police, and neighbors all acknowledge that legitimate violence, that is, violence of the authorities, was deployed. Of course, some do so with considerably more ambivalence than others. Legitimate violence is a violence that the official authorities claim to have domesticated and tamed with—what else—language. Language guides and controls the violence as orders are given, chains of command elaborated, guidelines for combat codified. Language of this very special sort obscures the fact that legitimate violence actually engages in violation.

Vietnam on Osage Avenue

Another strand of the discourse of war engaged both the metaphor and metonymy of Vietnam. A large number of official participants and neighborhood residents in this conflict had been in the military or in a war or in both. This figure comes from the spontaneous mention by or explicit soliciting of this information from witnesses at the MOVE hearings and those individuals quoted in the *Philadelphia Inquirer*. Figures on the military history of the entire personnel of the Philadelphia police officers have proven impossible to obtain. In any case, six police officers referred to having been in Vietnam, the military reserves, or other occasions of military combat. Five city administrators, including the mayor and the managing director, noted their military histories. Four fire fighters, including the commissioner, mentioned military service. Two MOVE commissioners and three residents of Osage Avenue and the surrounding neighborhood made similar references. Despite the almost accidental nature of this sample, it is striking that military biographical history even came up and that it did so frequently. The repeated surfacing of a seemingly irrelevant biographical detail alerted me to a certain thematic resonance—the MOVE confrontation was being framed as a war.

What were the components of this war? What kind of a war was it? Neighbors suggested that MOVE children could be wired with explosives as were children of the Vietcong. Officer Washington expressed a similar fear about apprehending a fire-fleeing Ramona Africa. Media reports of the day's events continuously made reference to a sensation neighbors had that they were back in Vietnam: "How do you like our Tet offensive?" asked one man of *Philadelphia Inquirer* columnist Dorothy Storck. "It's like a second Vietnam," said another neighborhood resident. A resident of nearby Pine Street was quoted as saying that the sight of his home reminded him of war: "They were still flushing the area out . . . I started to say 'VC.' They were still flushing out MOVE . . . It looked like some of the villages we used to level."[64] Even Mayor Goode, explaining his absence from the scene of May 13, claimed: "There have been, as I was told, instances of the fact that commanders in the Army have, in fact, been mistakenly shot."[65] And in editorials, columns, and news articles, the *Inquirer* made reference or quoted someone making reference to a "neighborhood burned down in what had been conceived as an effort to save it."

Why was the Vietnam War idiom so pervasive and so perversely natural? Ten years after that war was over, it continued, in however latent a form, to have a hold both on those who lived in the minority neighborhoods of people who had fought the war and on those who policed them. And what of the MOVE members themselves? They were not immune to its influence either. As Kathleen Neal Cleaver writes: "The adults in

MOVE had bought into the glorification of violence that suffused our society during the Vietnam war era. They were survivors and observers of the war psychosis that Vietnam brought to a boil in black ghettoes already seething with drug abuse, crime and family deterioration. At the same time, the police in the neighborhoods were recipients of the transfer of military tactics from Vietnam into domestic police action. These men in uniform, above all, brought the war home."[66]

The discourse of war, ultimately, did correspond to the degree of destruction on Osage Avenue on May 13. It did not, however, explain or justify it. For as much as the shadow and influence of Vietnam, and the military orientations of those officials whose lives had been so involved in military contexts and engagements, hung over the operation of Philadelphia police, the alternative discourses of sentiment, domesticity, bureaucracy, and negotiation interfered. They did so by interposing alternative images of MOVE, the neighborhood, the children, the responsibility of the city, and the very nature of the conflict itself. Thus in some ways the same lack of moral conviction that haunted the Vietnam War echoes through the Vietnam redux on Osage Avenue.

CHAPTER SIX

Decarcerating Discourse

Truth is restored by reducing the lie to an absurdity, but truth itself does not seek words; she is afraid to entangle herself in the word, to soil herself in verbal pathos.

Mikhail Bakhtin, *The Dialogic Imagination*

To speak the truth—a desire, an ambition, the presupposition of academic studies. The problem is that a study basing itself on the very notion that truth speaking is always tendentious, always incorporated in the body or bodies of discursive formations, cannot perform a magical unveiling of the "true" story at the end. I like Bakhtin's phrase "verbal pathos" because there is something pathetic about the crystallizing process of speech, the attempt to capture and define an opulent reality in words. But of course, we have little choice. Our options are to suspend disbelief in the shaping powers of speech and propose an "objective" official version of events, or to say nothing, or, as Bakhtin suggests, to restore truth through the back door of "reducing the lie to an absurdity." It is the third option that I have attempted in this book.

The methodological strategy of combing through the discursive surround of an event such as the MOVE conflict imagines a world of discourses that act as if they are self-contained and natural mirrors of their own worlds, but that are really bearers of their own incompletion and tendentiousness. Elected officials, city bureaucrats, police, West Philadelphia homeowners, lawyers, former MOVE members—all weave narratives of the MOVE/city/neighborhood conflict and of the horror of May 13, 1985, with their own vocabularies of motives and actions. All seek to encompass that reality in their speech, yet all come up, either consciously or unconsciously, against the limits of sayability within each separate discursive formation. I am not suggesting that a simple combinatory principle—add all the worldviews of all the discourses together and you get the truth—would solve the problem of partiality (a word I use here to mean both tendentiousness and fragmentation). In fact, it is quite clear that some discursive formations distinctly contradict others. Rather, I examine the material ramifications of particular moments of discursive couplings, borrowings, importations, and contaminations. The dream of narrative mimesis will forever remain elusive, but it is potentially our dissatisfaction at the partiality of the reigning discursive formations that can be the prod toward reducing the lie to an absurdity. And it is by attending to those gaps and interactions among discourses that such an analysis can be performed.

Emergent Discourses in the MOVE Conflict

In my analysis of the languages that talked the MOVE conflict into and through the particular shape it assumed, I have identified four major clusters of terms, or discursive formations. These four are discourses of bureaucracy, law, sentiment, and war. Each of these discourses contains a particular worldview that involves notions of what it is to be a human being and how human beings can and should interact. In one sense, these discourses seem self-contained; confronted in an official capacity with a social or political conflict, the lawyer or the bureaucrat brings only the discursive tools of his or her trade to bear on that conflict. A lawyer will traffic in criminal codes, arrest warrants, legal precedents, and so forth, not in God, salvation, and sin. But in another sense, these discourses inevitably acknowledge (grudgingly, ironically, respectfully, etc.) other discursive domains precisely by being diffident about addressing issues outside of their purview. This is an interesting and important paradox. How do you claim both autonomy and dependency at the same time? The variety of ways of enacting that paradox is key to understanding how certain dispute trajectories are either facilitated or prevented. Let us first look at how the city officials charged with resolving the MOVE conflict enacted that paradox.

At precise moments in the ongoing discursive flow of the MOVE conflict the officials in question referred to different discourses. The bureaucrat, for example, could refer to the discourse of religion. On August 9, 1984, after an actual brawl with MOVE member Frank Africa, one of the neighbors of MOVE, Lloyd Wilson, met with Managing Director Brooks and Police Commissioner Sambor to discuss the tension on the block. According to Wilson, after talking awhile, he asked if there were any official plans to deal with the situation. "After a long conversation, they said, 'Only an act of God could change this.'"[1] When asked to identify the speaker, Wilson indicated that it had been Brooks. Brooks was then asked, during his testimony at the MOVE hearings, to clarify his comments to Wilson: "And then as to the reference to God, I quite often, Mr. Lytton, express—make expressions about God. And I'm sure that my expression was probably more, 'This is a matter that we all need to take to God.' And I say that to people in crisis moments quite often in my professional life, as in my private life."[2] Similarly, Commissioner Sambor, when asked whether he believed an armed confrontation was inevitable, answered that probably yes, it was. Then a member of the MOVE commission asked him, "It was not your wish, I think you told Father Washington [another member of the MOVE commission], not your wish but it was your belief that that was what would happen? A. Not my wish sir. It was also my prayer that it would not occur."[3]

These references, or deferrals, to discursive domain outside of the purview of the official's control may strike us as ritualistic or insincere. Certainly, they seem to have struck Wilson as such. In this sense they seem insignificant, trivial, not at all what the larger text is about. I would argue that they are absolutely crucial, not so much in what they directly effected, but in what they reveal. Primarily, they reveal blank spots in the institutional discourse of the speakers. To the degree that the speakers themselves are willing and able to recognize these blank spots, they must admit to other discursive formations with all their attendant terms and worldviews. Attending to this "marginalia" is analytically important. Mine is a purposeful search for the marginal in the discursive surround of an event. This category includes unconscious leaks of one discourse into another (for example, metaphorical expressions used to explain actions or decisions that seem to turn the meanings of the actions on their heads or to send them in different interpretive directions—District Attorney Rendell's use of the term *ripen* to talk about what arrest warrants can do is one such moment); repetitions of terms with slight, seemingly insignificant variations (recall Fire Commissioner Richmond's statement that he was responsible for any fire fighter who turned off a hose line at the "bequest, the instruction, the request, the insinuation of a police officer"); and points of contact between one and another discourse (the above references to prayer and God are examples of one kind of interdiscourse contact). Such momentary "aberrations" in a given discursive performance reveal, I believe, conflicts, desires, intensities, and gaps that are either not or only inadvertently acknowledged. In this they can be key to understanding interactions among protagonists of a complex event.

Characterizing the Discourses

Of the four identified discursive formations, two are essentially means-oriented (bureaucratic and legal) and two are ends-oriented (sentimental and military) in terms of the ways they operated in this conflict. This is not to say that in a different context these discourses could not change their valences (legal discourse could reflect or establish the ends of a just society, equality, and so forth) or that there were not elements of means orientation in ends-oriented discourse even in this case (the discourse of war was swollen with notions and images of tactics and weaponry). Rather, positioning of these discourses relative to each other and to the public categorized them either as means or as ends. Thus the ends-oriented discourses of sentiment and war pointed in their separate ways to an ideal and an evil world. The sentimental language of children and innocence and neighbors making Santa Claus constructed an ideal, almost utopian, world of normalcy that, once disrupted by MOVE, cried out for restitution. The discourse of war established an image of an enemy and evil intent that demanded annihilation. The means-oriented discourses of bureaucracy and law declare their incompetence in the establishing of ends; they must import their ends from elsewhere. They provide the means for moving through the conflict. They establish chains of command, procedures for codifying arrest warrants, and tactical plans. They merely follow the rules.

Thus the discourses of bureaucracy and the law circled around the means, and the discourses of sentiment and war provided the ends. The problem is that these two sets of discourses, as deployed by the participants in this conflict, could not directly communicate with each other, making the relationship between means and ends full of gaps and leaps. Thus events like the bombing of the MOVE house and the use of the fire as a tactical weapon seemed to erupt, literally and figuratively, out of the long series of meetings and plans and protests and cautions. After analyzing the languages of these various occasions of meetings and so forth, it seems that there was a heavy weighting in the direction of means. The ends emerged only at unstable junctures, such as those moments when officials were actively figuring out what the children of MOVE were (hostages, combatants, deluded innocents). Imported in this way, such ends as sentimental salvation were coupled with practical abandonment. Perhaps it was such a coupling that gave meaning to Oscar Wilde's famous line, "It takes a hard man not to laugh at Little Nell's death."

The emergence, or eruption, of ends into discussions of means is an analytically significant moment when discussions of means predominate. Here such things as religion and emotion play a strange and defamiliarizing role. Recall Managing Director Brooks's statement, "I had an emotion." Emotion in this sense is a foreign object that finds itself in the middle of a means-oriented discourse. Similarly, the assistant district attorney's reference to the "subjunctive mood" of the district attorney's office strikes us as a strange thing to say about the legal business of prosecution. These importations seem unnatural and problematize simultaneously the dominant discourse of means and the other-worldly references. They reveal moments of discursive breakdown.

Discursive Breakdown and Its Relation to Violence

I use *discursive breakdown* to refer to contingent moments in a discourse when that discourse reaches some limit in what it can say. In other words, it reaches some limit (acknowledged or unacknowledged) in appropriating the world representationally. *Discursive breakdown* has, I am aware, psychoanalytic resonances. It should be clear, however, that any resonance with psychoanalytic methodology in this book assumes a social unconscious that works differentially through differentially positioned individuals, rather than an individual unconscious at work in society. In explicating an analysis of discourse that reads therein a social unconscious, and thus discursive breakdowns, I find literary critic Mary Poovey's explanation most useful: "The tropes of displacement, condensation, working through, repression and symbolic action seem appropriate to the transmigrations and transvaluations of the images and themes . . . in these texts." Thus she is particularly interested in "the ways in which [clusters of associated images] combine or exchange terms with other associated clusters of images, and the extent to which they provide the vehicle in which thematic issues can be worked through by means of the symbolic resolution of contradictions or the management of destabilizing tensions. This is a structural psychoanalytic methodology in the sense that I interpret the organizational principles governing the production of meaning and not the individual characters or writers."[4]

Beyond the moments of importation of foreign images and expressions in the MOVE hearings, two forms of discursive breakdown are particularly interesting. The first is silence, both literal silence and "I don't know" as an answer to a question. Recall the former MOVE member's characterization of Mayor Goode as a man who "listens, but doesn't say much," when referring to their meetings in the early eighties.

Commissioner Sambor was asked if "there was any notice given to those people whose houses you felt might well be damaged that, in fact, their houses might be damaged and they should take with them any precious personal belongings." Sambor answered simply, "No, sir." When asked why not, he responded, "I don't know."[5] From within the discursive world of the tactical and bureaucratic languages of the police commissioner, there is simply no way to explain the absence of practical concern for the domestic belongings of the neighbors. Even while deferring to the rhetoric of sentiment and domesticity in mandating ends, there is no natural way to incorporate sentimental salvation into military tactics and no natural way to explain its nonoccurrence. The discourse breaks down with feeble gestures to things that cannot be said.

The second form of discursive breakdown appears to be the opposite of the silence of the first—that is, discursive excess, the proliferation, repetition, exaggeration, extremism of terms. Examples of such excess are abundant in the MOVE conflict. Transcripts of MOVE on the loudspeaker reveal the word *motherfucker* three or four times in any sentence. Similarly, threats were deployed liberally: traffic in many major European cities will be tied up, many politicians will have their heads blown in. The terminological excess of MOVE was well matched by that of the city officials: Goode's fragmenting and multiplying himself into mayor, human being, parent, person, and the commissioner's reference to "the bequest, the instruction, the request, the insinuation of a police officer." Notions of identity—of the self and of given speech acts—are here largely indeterminate, and the speaker spins out of control coming up with terms to grasp them.

How do such discursive breakdowns in ongoing disputes structurally relate to the possibility of the occurrence of violence? Elaine Scarry has arrived at something crucial in her *Body in Pain.* Her entire book is preoccupied with the ways in which bodily pain is and isn't made visible in language. At one point she takes up the question of the discursive representations of moments of transition from peace to war.

> Clausewitz's famous dictum, "War is the continuation of politics by other means," achieves its authority and authenticity in the brilliant ease of assertion with which a complicated and elusive phenomenon is suddenly made to stand before one as though it had always been self-evident. Nevertheless, it is a statement which, when cited in isolation, as it so often is, sometimes seems to assert that "war is the continuation of peace (or peacetime activities) by other means" and thus to ally and elide it with a benign activity. Its continuity with

peace, the predicate nominative, grammatically dominates the "by other means" of injuring . . . Dying is living only different; bleeding is breathing only not exactly. (p. 77).

Scarry's point is that official discourse regarding the move from peace to war elides the very transformation that has occurred and thus makes war appear a much less harmful (shall we follow Goode and conflate *harmful* and *fatal* here?) activity. Similarly, something in the ongoing, enacting, official discourse must have paved the way for such a transformation to take place. And perhaps analogous to the post hoc representational discourse of denial that Scarry charts, this preparatory discourse performs a similar elision. The forms this elision takes are those of discursive breakdown. Silence and terminological promiscuity both, in their way, point to a kind of abandonment of speech, a loss of faith in its power to control a situation, the world. And violence can flow into that gap.

Of course, violence doesn't just fall from the sky into the discursive fissures of official authorities. Concrete discursive steps are followed in particular types of disputes. In the MOVE conflict, threats of neighbor vigilante violence added to symbolic transformations of the MOVE house into a "compound" with a "bunker," and to the kinds of official discursive breakdowns I have charted push in the direction of official violence. The moment of transition from peace to war could indeed be calibrated in terms of the various hand offs of authority in which new discourses took over from old. The bureaucrats handed off to the lawyers, the lawyers handed off to the police, the police handed off to the bomb squad and the stake-out teams. At each moment terms of understanding and world appropriation shifted; at each moment the relation of means and ends was altered until, with the charge to bring essentially anything and everything in the way of weaponry to the scene, and a similarly discursively frozen opponent in MOVE, violence was inevitable. From this perspective, the issue should not be who fired the first shot.

Ways Out

It is hard for humans to accept such inevitability of death and destruction. We look for ways out, ways to forestall violence in disputes. My contribution to such a search, based largely on the research carried out in this study, involves theorizing a difference in the modes of discursive interaction. The basic theory is that there are two poles of interaction, contamination and hybridization. Contamination involves discursive eruptions that reveal the dependency of a given discursive formation on alternative discursive formations. For example, the rules-bound, hierarchical, universalistic, disinterested discourse of bureaucracy has proven to be dependent upon the private and interested discourse of sentimentality when bureaucracy must articulate its actions to the outside world. Similarly, the discourse of war has shown itself to be dependent on the images from a domestic discursive economy (tear gas = powdered milk). But the dependency is revealed only in so-called marginal moments, in socially unconscious leaks in texts and speeches, and is thus unacknowledged as critical, essential. It happens, as it were, behind the backs of the very speakers. Hybridization, on the other hand, means a practical acknowledgment of the incompleteness, the partiality of a given discursive formation. This involves discursive self-critique and an openness to other discourses. The constant aim of hybridization is the deinstitutionalization of discourse. This involves a continual enactment of the fact that, as Bakhtin writes, "it frequently happens that even one and the same word will belong simultaneously to two languages, two belief systems that intersect in a hybrid construction."[6] Those speakers engaged in discursive hybridization are structurally similar to those social agents of whom Foucault wrote, such as the professionally oriented yet subordinate care-giver nurse, who are in contradictory locations in disciplinary power formations. These agents have the metaphorical taste of two discursive worlds in their mouths, and their knowledge is "local," not completely caught up in the institutional relations of power, not completely constructed either as "in charge" or as "incarcerated." In the MOVE conflict the organic mediators occupied such a position. They had the discursive flexibility to move back and forth across several discursive formations, to self-consciously cobble together speech acts through borrowings and reframings. Simply, they gave themselves the license to be creative. Of course, they were unsuccessful.

It is necessary to clarify the issue of intentionality in relation to the difference between contamination and hybridization. In either process the speakers of the discourses may or may not be conscious of manipulating language to their own assessed interests. While this may be important in studies of political strategy, I refer here to a different kind of stance toward discourse, that which Hollway calls "taking up a position within a discourse." Such stances are ultimately more a construct of one's position in the institutional structures of society than a conscious attitude toward what one thinks an audience would want to hear.

If the opposition between contamination and hybridization corresponds to the possibilities of, on the one hand, discursive breakdown and, on the other hand, discursive deinstitutionalization, clearly it would be in our interest to figure out how to provide for more of the latter. Here it might be useful to look once again at the notion of being a witness. What does it mean to be a witness to an event, to bear witness? Are there different species of witness—privileged and underprivileged types? Who gets to say what in critical social moments?

We have already seen that in the Watergate hearings certain witnesses were asked certain kinds of questions in certain ways. Similarly, for the Iran-Contra hearings, Bogen and Lynch show "how the witness [Oliver North] is able to resist the movement from biography to history by embedding his stories with a set of local entitlements that resist translation into a generalized narrative."[7] There are clearly privileged witnesses who, for structural, ideological, and political reasons, are asked only certain kinds of questions and permitted certain kinds of responses. Let us imagine an alternative universe in which city officials, say, along with Birdie Africa/Michael Moses Ward, would be asked if they know what it means to tell the truth; and along with city leaders, MOVE neighbors and former MOVE members would be asked explicitly to recall their emotions and chart their force, rather than simply have it assumed that they experienced them. Such a world would seem topsy-turvy to us, used to certain kinds of question-answer sequences and social role insulations.

Such possibilities of alternative sets of questions are similar to an issue posed by Conley and O'Barr in their study of the ethnography of legal discourse. "Are there 'folk' approaches to narration that are being frustrated by court procedures? Are there any consistencies in the way that lay litigants would structure legal accounts in the absence of evidentiary constraints?"[8] One might term the relentlessly deinstitutionalized testimony of the organic mediators a "folk approach." One crucial aspect of that narrative approach is consistent disinterestedness in the process of categorization. Witnesses bound up in institutional discourses, by contrast, are continually preoccupied with categories: who is in charge, who is a criminal, what kind of crime, and—the biggest question of all—what is MOVE? The compulsion to categorize preempts a bricolagelike creativity. This study has demonstrated many instances of such preemption. Thus in the sense that their testimony, both during and after the conflict itself, received essentially no response, the organic mediators might well be termed underprivileged witnesses.

Our Terror

No criminal indictments were ever handed down to any city official involved in the MOVE horror of May 13, 1985, despite two grand jury investigations (although the city of Philadelphia has paid approximately $24 million in civil suit fines to MOVE members regarding the children). Something terrible happened on that day to many people, but the event was somehow swallowed, like a nightmare, by the society that allowed it to occur. I believe that the event and its swallowing refract, in a particular way, our terror of the inchoate. As in the distinction between categorizing discourses (subject to contamination) and category-disinterested discourses (prone to hybridization), MOVE itself comes to represent the intolerable inchoate. All civilizations have a form of terror at the inchoate, the unknowable. Some call them demons, some witches, and some—ours—terrorists. Clearly, MOVE was frightening, adamant, at times oppressive, definitely a bad neighbor. But I am not in the business of locating blame, but of recounting and interpreting stories. As Sue Wells argues in her analysis of the MOVE commission report, it is important to note not only stories that cohere but also those that don't: "The report reproduces the resistance of the MOVE catastrophe to being known, normalized, or reduced to an official story. Paradoxically, it is the gaps and inconsistencies that make the document both unsatisfying and powerful, since it is the very resistance to being normalized that is important in the story of MOVE."[9]

This is a story about homes and children and honest citizens caught in the thralldom of the obscene, the evil. It is a sentimental story that seeks to deny that evil and violence and obscenity can thrive as much in the home as outside of it. It is a story of a "rational" bureaucracy that fixated on control and that "desired" but avoided knowing a tactical plan to arrest criminals. It is a story of "honest citizens" held hostage as much by their rescuers (who punch holes in their walls, explode the fronts of their houses, don't advise them to take their possessions with them, and allow a fire to burn down their homes) as by the antisystem group that used them as political bait.

On the other side, as in some surrealistic painting of melting clocks, it is a story of a house that underwent a strange transformation. It grew a bunker; the doors and windows were boarded up with logs. It was a house that was itself in a state of terror. It was a house with children, those mythical creatures of this romance about civilization. But if this house was no longer a home, perhaps the children were only "children," and a bomb could break the spell.

The plethora of stories here demonstrates, finally, the critical importance of language in this conflict. I have attempted, in this book, to build theory via the close examination of a particular case with the tool of discourse analysis. Perhaps such theory might help chart a path through the discursive forest of rationalities, excesses, silence, and incoherence by purposely examining the intertwining of the trees.

NOTES

Chapter One

1. Scarry explored these issues in depth in her provocative and brilliant work, *The Body in Pain*.

2. Gerth and Mills, quoted in Brown, *Society as Text*, p. 56.

3. Pratt, "Linguistic Utopias," p. 60.

4. Goffman, *Fame Analysis*, p. 12.

5. For elaboration of these various conversation-analysis notions, see the following, among others: Sacks, Schegloff, and Jefferson, "A Simplest Systematics for the Organization of Turn-taking in Conversation," and Ervin-Tripp, "On Sociolinguistic Rules."

6. An exception to this rule is the extremely interesting article on the Watergate hearings by Molotch and Boden, "Talking Social Structure," pp. 273–88.

7. Wilson, "Social Structure and Interaction," in Boden and Zimmerman, *Talk and Social Structure*, p. 22.

8. Emanuel A. Schegloff, "Reflections on Talk and Social Structure," in Boden and Zimmerman, *Talk and Social Structure*, p. 50.

9. Wagner-Pacifici and Schwartz, "The Vietnam Veterans Memorial," p. 383.

10. Bakhtin, *Speech Genres*, p. 84.

11. Burke, *A Grammar of Motives*, p. 74.

12. Goodrich, *Legal Discourse*, pp. 132, 144.

13. Ibid., p. 91.

14. Wendy Hollway, "Gender Difference and the Production of Subjectivity," in Henriques et al., *Changing the Subject*, p. 236.

15. Carol Cohn, personal communication.

16. Bakhtin, *Speech Genres*, p. 79.

17. Robert Sanders, "Discursive Constraints on the Acceptance and Rejection of Knowledge Claims: The Conversation about Conversation," in Simons, *The Rhetorical Turn*, p. 150.

18. Hollway, *Changing the Subject*, p. 238.

19. This being Mannheim's paradox, as well as one largely unacknowledged by Foucault, I'll simply identify it as a problem.

20. Jameson, *The Political Unconscious*, p. 60.

21. Bakhtin, *The Dialogic Imagination*, p. 348.

22. Griswold, "A Methodological Framework for the Sociology of Culture," pp. 1–35.

23. Keiser, "The Rise of a Biracial Coalition in Philadelphia," p. 56.

24. Goode, *In Goode Faith*, p. 181.

25. Karnig and Welch, *Black Representation and Urban Policy*, p. 112.

26. Cf. Wilson, *The Truly Disadvantaged*, for a detailed analysis of the macrostructural aspects of this transformation.

27. MOVE, *Twenty Years on the MOVE*, p. 6. One particularly interesting feature of this 1992 publication is the total absence of profanity in the entire historical narrative. At this point at least, MOVE is quite clear about the contextuated uses of language.

28. All of the listed materials, thanks largely to the work of the Special Investigation Commission, are in the public domain, and many of them are housed in Temple University's Urban Archives Collection.

29. Bogen and Lynch, "Taking Account of the Hostile Native," p. 203.

30. Danet, "Language in the Legal Process," p. 514.

31. Molotch and Boden, "Talking Social Structure," p. 273.

32. Ibid.

33. Danet, "Language in the Legal Process," p. 522.

34. Louise James, Philadelphia Special Investigation Commission Hearings, 10/10/85 A.M., p. 24. All further references to these hearings will read "MOVE Commission Hearings."

Chapter Two

1. The term is overly general, decontextuates action, and refers more to effects and ideologies than to specific organizations and acts. If pressed, I tend to follow Richard Rubenstein's definition of terrorism: "politically motivated violence engaged in by small groups claiming to represent the masses" (*Alchemists of Revolution*, p. xvi).

2. Cleaver, "Philadelphia Fire," p. 151.

3. Cf. particularly Assefa and Wahrhaftig, *Extremist Groups and Conflict Resolution*.

4. McCoy, "Who Was John Africa?" p. 18.

5. Excerpt from interview with Powelton Village community activist, carried out by student researcher Heidi Feldman.

6. Cox, "My Life in MOVE," pp. 170–2.

7. Assefa and Wahrhaftig, *Extremist Groups and Conflict Resolution*, p. 22.

8. Laverne Sims, MOVE Commission Hearings, 10/9/85 P.M. p. 104.

9. John Cresci, MOVE Commission Hearings, 10/8/85 A.M., p. 32.

10. Bennie Swans, MOVE Commission Hearings, 10/9/85 P.M., p. 38.

11. Anderson and Hevenor, *Burning Down the House*, p. 284.

12. Gregor Sambor, MOVE Commission Hearings, 10/17/85 P.M., p. 199.

13. Excerpt from MOVE group statement to Philadelphia police force, May 20, 1977.

14. Bennie Swans, MOVE Commission Hearings, 10/9/85 P.M., p. 45.

15. George Draper, MOVE Commission Hearings, 10/8/85 P.M., p. 14.

16. Louise James, MOVE Commission Hearings, 10/10/85 A.M., pp. 65–68.

17. McCoy, "Who Was John Africa?" p. 24.

18. Excerpt from interview with Powelton Village community activist carried out by student researcher Heidi Feldman.

19. Assefa and Wahrhaftig, *Extremist Groups and Conflict Resolution*, lists groups and their positions on pp. 29–33.

20. Wilson Goode, MOVE Commission Hearings, 10/11/85 P.M., pp. 85–95.

21. MOVE, *Twenty Years on the MOVE*, p. 40.

22. "The Findings, Conclusions, and Recommendations of the Philadelphia Special Investigation Commission," p. 19.

23. Nagel, "Psychological Obstacles to Administrative Responsibility," p. 6.

24. Philadelphia Special Investigation Commission files 453 and 454.

25. See "MOVE Members at the Osage Avenue House Have Contended That Their Actions Are Political, *Philadelphia Inquirer*, May 13, 1985, p. 5A; see also Thad Mathis, "A Political Analysis of the So-Called "MOVE" Tragedy: Preliminary Examination of Black Power and Municipal Decision-Making under Crisis," in seminar proceedings sponsored by American Friends Service Committee, To Create a More Perfect Union: Lessons from the MOVE Tragedy, March 1987.

26. Robert Williams, MOVE Commission Hearings, 10/22/85 P.M., p. 25.

27. Transcript from United States District Court for the Eastern District of Pennsylvania, July 2, 1981, *United States of America vs. Vincent Leaphart, a/k/a John Africa, Alphonso Robbins*, Criminal Action no. 77-380, pp. 1.3–1.5, 1.4–1.6.

28. Lloyd Wilson, MOVE Commission Hearings, 10/9/85 A.M., pp. 36–37.

29. Ibid., p. 94.

30. "Mayor Calls Situation with MOVE 'Explosive,'" *Philadelphia Inquirer*, May 9, 1985, p. 6B.

31. Carrie Foskey, MOVE Commission Hearings, 10/8/85 P.M., p. 107.

32. "MOVE House Stirs Neighbors' Anger," *Philadelphia Inquirer*, May 2, 1985, p. 1B.

33. Walter Washington, MOVE Commission Hearings, 11/1/85 A.M., pp. 68–70.

34. Anderson and Hevenor, *Burning Down the House*, p. 274.

35. "Mayor Calls Situation with MOVE 'Explosive,'" *Philadelphia Inquirer*, May 5, 1985, p. 6B.

36. "Talk, Settlement Hopes Foundered on Issue of Future Arrests," *Philadelphia Inquirer*, May 14, 1985, p. 12A.

37. Louise James, MOVE Commission Hearings, 10/10/85 A.M., pp. 43–44.

38. Laverne Sims, MOVE Commission Hearings, 10/9/85 P.M., p. 92.

39. *United States of American vs. Vincent Leaphart,* p. 2.139.

40. Philadelphia Special Investigation Commission Records.

41. Louise James, MOVE Commission Hearings, 10/9/85 P.M., pp. 126–27.

42. Philadelphia Special Investigation Commission Records.

43. Louise James, MOVE Commission Hearings, 10/9/85 P.M., p. 123.

44. Ibid., p. 124.

45. Laverne Sims, MOVE Commission Hearings, 10/9/85 P.M., p. 139.

46. Stallybrass, "Marx and Heterogeneity," p. 72.

47. "No Automatic Weapons Reported in MOVE Search," *Philadelphia Inquirer,* May 18, 1985, p. 8A.

48. Gregor Sambor, MOVE Commission Hearings, 10/18/85 P.M., p. 156.

Chapter Three

1. *Webster's Ideal Dictionary* (Springfield, Mass.: G. and C. Merriam Co., 1961).

2. See my discussion of melodrama in social-political life in *The Moro Morality Play,* pp. 278–83.

3. Brooks, *The Melodramatic Imagination;* Tompkins, *Sensational Designs;* Fisher, *Hard Facts;* Sanchez-Eppler, "Bodily Bonds."

4. Nedelsky, "Laws, Boundaries, and the Bounded Self," p. 177.

5. Bellingham, "The Unspeakable Blessing," p. 307.

6. Arendt, *The Human Condition,* p. 71.

7. Brown, "Foreword to the Report of the Philadelphia Special Investigation Commission," pp. 267–69.

8. Bowser, "The Philadelphia Special Investigation Commission" p. 388.

9. Brown, *Society as Text,* pp. 29, 32–33.

10. Betty Mapp, MOVE Commission Hearings, 10/9/85 A.M., p. 4.

11. Ibid., pp. 5, 7.

12. Cassandra Carter, MOVE Commission Hearings, 10/9/85 A.M., p. 55.

13. Lucretia Wilson, MOVE Commission Hearings, 10/9/85 A.M., p. 88.

14. Cassandra Carter, MOVE Commission Hearings, 10/9/85 A.M., p. 32.

15. Ibid., p. 68.

16. Laverne Sims, MOVE Commission Hearings, 10/9/85 P.M., p. 95.

17. Anderson and Hevenor, *Burning Down the House,* p. 243.

18. Birdie Africa, MOVE Commission Hearings, 10/31/85 P.M., pp. 295–98.

19. Anderson and Hevenor, *Burning Down the House,* p. 261.

20. Zelizer, *Pricing the Priceless Child,* p. 15.

21. Wilson Goode, MOVE Commission Hearings, 10/11/85 P.M., p. 107.

22. Clifford Bond, MOVE Commission Hearings, 10/9/85 P.M., pp. 17–18.

23. Betty Mapp, MOVE Commission Hearings, 10/9/85 A.M., pp. 37–38.

24. Wilson Goode, MOVE Commission Hearings, 10/11/85 P.M., p. 55.

25. Gregor Sambor, MOVE Commission Hearings, 10/17/85 A.M., pp. 28–29.

26. Leo Brooks, MOVE Commission Hearings, 10/10/85 A.M., pp. 55–56.

27. Wilson Goode, MOVE Commission Hearings, 10/11/85 P.M., p. 49.

28. Ibid., p. 50.

29. American Friends Service Committee, *Voices from the Community*, p. 15.

30. Inez Nichols, MOVE Commission Hearings, 10/8/85 P.M., p. 110.

31. Cassandra Carter, MOVE Commission Hearings, 10/9/85 A.M., pp. 48–49.

32. Gregor Sambor, MOVE Commission Hearings, 10/17/85 A.M., p. 151.

33. There has been considerable debate about whether this back alley was also the site of police officers' shooting at MOVE members who attempted to escape. Neither the MOVE Special Investigation Commission nor a Philadelphia County Special Investigating Grand Jury ever developed enough evidence of this to charge anyone. For more on this see Boyette and Boyette, *"Let It Burn."*

34. James Berghaier, MOVE Commission Hearings, 11/1/85 A.M., pp. 110–18.

35. Walter Washington, MOVE Commission Hearings, 11/1/85 A.M., p. 22.

36. David Shrager, lawyer for Birdie Africa/Michael Moses Ward, MOVE Commission Hearings, 10/31/85 P.M., pp. 206–13.

37. Birdie Africa/Michael Moses Ward, MOVE Commission Hearings, 10/31/85 P.M., pp. 231, 359–60.

38. Capuzzo "The Miracle of Birdie Africa," pp. 16, 17, 29.

39. Collins, "Three Faces of Cruelty," p. 417.

40. De Sousa Santos, "The Law of the Oppressed," pp. 80–81.

41. Ibid., p. 82.

42. United Residents of the Sixty-two Hundred Block of Osage Avenue to Governor Thornburgh, March 8, 1985, MOVE Commission Files, Urban Archives Collection, Temple University.

43. Bracy, *Making Them Whole*, p. 14.

44. Bowser, *Let the Bunker Burn*, p. 76.

45. United Residents to Thornburgh.

46. Bowser, *Let the Bunker Burn*, p. 71.

47. Laverne Sims, MOVE Commission Hearings, 10/9/85 P.M., p. 128.

48. Nathan Foskey, MOVE Commission Hearings, 10/8/85 P.M., pp. 115–6.

49. Stern, "A Pluralistic Reading of the First Amendment," p. 931.

50. Louise James, MOVE Commission Hearings, 10/10/85 A.M., pp. 43–44.

51. For the slipperiness and complication of class, one exemplary study is that of David Halle, *America's Working Man*. In this ethnography of chemical-factory workers, Halle discovers a kind of split identity: working-class at the point of production, middle-class at the point of consumption.

As for race, the historian Barbara Jeanne Fields has sought to refute this concept's ontological stability, claiming that race is not an element of human biology but rather an ideology. See "Slavery, Race, and Ideology in the United States of America."

52. American Friends Service Committee, *Voices from the Community*, pp. 37–38.

53. Thad Mathis, "The Politics of MOVE," lecture at American Friends Service Committee, September 14, 1988.

54. Novella Williams, MOVE Commission Hearings, 10/22/85 P.M., pp. 5–6.

55. Lucien Blackwell, MOVE Commission Hearings, 10/22/85 P.M., p. 101.

56. Gerald Renfew, "Lessons from the MOVE Tragedy: Unfinished Business, Four Years Later," speech given at American Friends Service Committee Human Rights Day Forum, May 1989, Philadelphia.

57. Arendt, *The Human Condition*, p. 40.

58. Sacks "On Doing 'Being Ordinary,'" pp. 414, 418.

59. Clifford Bond, MOVE Commission Hearings, 10/9/85 P.M., p. 17.

60. Cassandra Carter, MOVE Commission Hearings, 10/9/85 A.M., p. 73.

61. Dreyfus and Rabinow, *Michel Foucault: Beyond Structuralism and Hermeneutics*, p. 158, quoting from *Discipline and Punish*.

62. Ibid., p. 159.

Chapter Four

1. Dentith, "Political Economy, Fiction, and the Language of Practical Ideology in Nineteenth-Century England," p. 186.

2. For the complete Weberian typology of bureaucracy, see his essay "Bureaucracy" in *From Max Weber*.

3. Ibid., p. 214.

4. Ibid., p. 231.

5. Levine, *The Flight from Ambiguity*, p. 169.

6. Nagel, "Psychological Obstacles to Administrative Responsibility," p. 18.

7. Ferguson, *The Feminist Case against Bureaucracy*, p. 131.

8. Aberbach et al., *Bureaucrats and Politicians in Western Democracies*, p. 16.

9. Gregor Sambor, MOVE Commission Hearings, 10/18/85 P.M., pp. 142–43.

10. Lerman, "Dominant Discourse," p. 77.

11. Blau, "The Study of Formal Organization," p. 60.

12. Frug, "The Ideology of Bureaucracy in American Law," pp. 1290–91.

13. Levine, *The Flight from Ambiguity*, p. 157, 158.

14. Susan Wells in her brilliant essay on the narrative construction of the final report of the MOVE commission notes that the system of reason in this report is that of instrumental reason. She refers to the work of Horkheimer and Adorno as providing an analytic frame for her analysis of this form of thought, a form calculating the world as an object of control

("Narrative Figures and Subtle Persuasions: The Rhetoric of the MOVE Report," in Simons, *The Rhetorical Turn*, p. 220).

15. Levine, *The Flight from Ambiguity*, p. 178.

16. Ferguson, *The Feminist Case against Bureaucracy*, p. 128.

17. Wilson Goode, MOVE Commission Hearings, 10/11/85 P.M., pp. 9–10.

18. Molotch and Boden, "Talking Social Structure."

19. Leo Brooks, MOVE Commission Hearings, 10/16/85 A.M., pp. 19–21.

20. Rudolph Paliaga, MOVE Commission Hearings, 10/11/85 A.M.

21. Barbara Mather, MOVE Commission Hearings, 10/22/85 P.M., pp. 128–29.

22. Bennie Swans, MOVE Commission Hearings, 10/9/85 P.M., p. 65.

23. Gregor Sambor, MOVE Commission Hearings, 10/17/85 A.M., p. 33. Peter Manning notes that police plans are generally not written or codified: "Unlike an army or a corporation, the police rarely set down written objectives, rarely have planning or research and development units, and are quite sensitive to short term shifts in political power. They prefer action to planning" ("The Police," p. 24).

24. Wells, "Narrative Figures and Subtle Persuasions," p. 222.

25. Wilson Goode, MOVE Commission Hearings, 10/11/85 P.M., pp. 21–22.

26. Leo Brooks, MOVE Commission Hearings, 10/16/85 A.M., pp. 5–6.

27. Wilson Goode, MOVE Commission Hearings, 10/11/85 P.M., pp. 86–87, 96.

28. Ibid., p. 32.

29. Weber, "Politics as a Vocation," in *From Max Weber*, p. 78.

30. Joseph O'Neil, MOVE Commission Hearings, 10/8/85 A.M., p. 69.

31. Gregor Sambor, MOVE Commission Hearings, 10/17/85 A.M., p. 5.

32. John Craig, MOVE Commission Hearings, 10/23/85 P.M., pp. 32–33.

33. Collins, "Three Faces of Cruelty," p. 432.

34. I am using the term *bomb* here with the sense that any explosive dropped from a helicopter is a bomb. However, this term evoked much debate and protest from the participants in the assault. That debate is detailed in chapter 5.

35. William Richmond, MOVE Commission Hearings, 10/30/85 A.M., p. 24.

36. Charles King, MOVE Commission Hearings, 11/5/85 A.M., p. 90.

37. Gregor Sambor, MOVE Commission Hearings, 10/18/85 A.M., pp. 74–77.

38. Wilson Goode, MOVE Commission Hearings, 10/15/85 P.M., p. 17.

39. Ibid., pp. 94–95.

40. American Friends Service Committee, *Voices from the Community*, p. 45.

41. Leo Brooks, MOVE Commission Hearings, 10/16/85 A.M., p. 79.

42. William Richmond, MOVE Commission Hearings, 10/30/85 A.M., pp. 95–96.

43. Louise James, MOVE Commission Hearings, 10/9/85 P.M., pp. 79–80.

44. "Rouse, Other Developers Submit Preliminary Plans for Rebuilding," *Philadelphia Inquirer*, May 17, 1985, p. 25A.

45. "Fire Is One of the Worst in Philadelphia's History," *Philadelphia Inquirer*, May 14, 1985, p. 12A.

Chapter Five

1. Cover, "Violence and the Word," pp. 1607–8, 1623.
2. Anderson and Hevenor, *Burning Down the House*, p. 197.
3. Ericson and Shearing, "The Scientification of Police Work," p. 129.
4. Clifford Bond, MOVE Commission Hearings, 10/9/85 P.M., p. 5.
5. Anderson and Hevenor, *Burning Down the House*, p. 280.
6. Ericson and Shearing, "The Scientification of Police Work," p. 132.
7. Frank Rossi, *Philadelphia Inquirer*, May 24, 1985, p. 14A.
8. James Shanahan, MOVE Commission Hearings, 10/23/85 A.M., p. 108.
9. MacAloon, "Steroids and the State," p. 20.
10. Boyette and Boyette, *Let It Burn*, pp. 303–4.
11. Novella Williams, MOVE Commission Hearings, 10/22/85 P.M., p. 60.
12. Police information report, April 1985, Philadelphia Special Investigation Commission Records.
13. Leo Brooks, MOVE Commission Hearings, 10/16/85 A.M., p. 26.
14. Danet, Hoffman, and Kermish, "Threats to the Life of the President," p. 185.
15. Edward Rendell, MOVE Commission Hearings, 10/22/85 A.M., p. 6, 8.
16. Cf. Harold Garfinkle, "'Good' Organizational Reasons for 'Bad' Clinic Records," in Turner, *Ethnomethodology*, pp. 109–127.
17. Eric Henson and Edward Rendell, MOVE Commission Hearings, 10/22/85 A.M., p. 9, 19.
18. Wilson Goode, MOVE Commission Hearings, 10/15/85 A.M., p. 14.
19. Cassandra Carter, MOVE Commission Hearings, 10/9/85 A.M., pp. 26–28.
20. "Talk, Settlement Hopes Foundered on Issue of Future Arrests," *Philadelphia Inquirer*, May 14, 1985, p. 12A.
21. Grayson, "The Warrant Clause in Historical Context," p. 113.
22. Edward Rendell, MOVE Commission Hearings, 10/22/85 A.M., p. 34.
23. Conley and O'Barr, *Rules versus Relationships*, p. ix.
24. Mather and Yngvesson, "Language, Audience, and the Transformation of Disputes," p. 781.
25. John White, Sr., MOVE Commission Hearings, 10/10/85 P.M., pp. 44–45.
26. Bennie Swans, MOVE Commission Hearings, 10/9/85 P.M., p. 36.
27. Bowser, *Let the Bunker Burn*, p. 77.
28. Ibid., p. 11.
29. Gregor Sambor, MOVE Commission Hearings, 10/18/85 A.M., pp. 28–29.

30. Novella Williams, MOVE Commission Hearings, 10/22/85 P.M., p. 53.

31. Mather and Yngvesson, "Language, Audience, and the Transformation of Disputes," p. 778.

32. "Talks, Settlement Hopes Foundered on Issue of Future Arrests," *Philadelphia Inquirer*, May 14, 1985, p. 1.

33. Bennie Swans to Mayor Wilson Goode June 18, 1985, MOVE Commission Files, Urban Archives Collection, Temple University.

34. Bennie Swans, MOVE Commission Hearings, 10/9/85 P.M., p. 60.

35. Assefa and Wahrhaftig, *Extremist Groups and Conflict Resolution*, quoting Sister Falakah Fatah, p. 69.

36. Goodrich, *Legal Discourse*, p. 190.

37. Novella Williams, MOVE Commission Hearings, 10/22/85 P.M., pp. 3–8.

38. Charles Burrus, MOVE Commission Hearings, 10/22/85 P.M., pp. 10, 16, 41.

39. Charles Burrus, MOVE Commission Hearings, 10/22/85 P.M., p. 66. What Conley and O'Barr have written about judiciary trials and their rules of evidence is relevant for these investigative hearings as well: "Except in the case of expert witnesses, the law of evidence expresses a strong preference for concrete descriptive testimony. Lay opinions, conclusions and generalizations are not necessarily impermissible but they are frequently restricted on the grounds that they are incompetent and/or not relevant to the issues at hand" (*Rules versus Relationships*, p. 17).

40. Charles Burrus, MOVE Commission Hearings, 10/22/85 P.M., p. 57.

41. Novella Williams, MOVE Commission Hearings, 10/22/85 P.M., p. 43.

42. Pratt, "Linguistic Utopias," p. 59.

43. Louise James, MOVE Commission Hearings, 10/10/85 A.M., pp. 9–13.

44. Sacks, "On Doing 'Being Ordinary,'" p. 421.

45. American Friends Service Committee, *Voices from the Community*, p. 32.

46. Swett, "Cultural Bias in the American Legal System," p. 81.

47. For a much more detailed study of the Philadelphia police force in the seventies and eighties, see the forthcoming study by Jack Greene.

48. Nagel, "Psychological Obstacles to Administrative Responsibility," p. 16.

49. William Brown III, "Affirmative Action in Philadelphia: It Has Worked," in Urban League of Philadelphia, *The State of Black Philadelphia*, p. 12.

50. Bowser, *Let the Bunker Burn*, p. 109, quoting Neil Shanahan.

51. Rubinstein, *City Police*, p. 324.

52. Jerome Skolnick, in Ermer and Strange, *Blacks and Bureaucracy*, p. 76.

53. Walter Washington, MOVE Commission Hearings, 11/1/85 A.M., p. 23.

54. Elliot Currie, in Platt, *The Politics of Riot Commissions*, p. 455.

55. Manning, "On the Phenomenology of Violence," p. 3.

56. Rubinstein, *City Police*, p. 271.

57. Platt, *The Politics of Riot Commissions*, p. 364.

58. Albert Revel, MOVE Commission Hearings, 10/24/85 A.M., p. 47.

59. Wilson Goode, MOVE Commission Hearings, 10/15/85 A.M., pp. 73–75.

60. John Craig, MOVE Commission Hearings, 10/23/85 A.M., p. 75.

61. Cohn, "Sex and Death in the Rational World of Defense Intellectuals," p. 691.

62. Leo Brooks, MOVE Commission Hearings, 10/16/85 P.M., p. 178.

63. Edward McLaughlin, MOVE Commission Hearings, 10/23/85 P.M., pp. 97–98.

64. "A Temple Dormitory Becomes a Haven for Many of the Homeless," *Philadelphia Inquirer*, May 15, 1985, p. 17A.

65. Wilson Goode, MOVE Commission Hearings, 10/15/85 A.M. Goode has subsequently claimed that he had been warned by close advisors not to go to the scene because "unknown members of my own police force had targeted me for death if I came near 62nd and Osage Avenue" (*In Goode Faith*, pp. 217–218).

66. Cleaver, "Philadelphia Fire," p. 156.

Chapter Six

1. Lloyd Wilson, MOVE Commission Hearings, 10/9/85 A.M., p. 96.

2. Leo Brooks, MOVE Commission Hearings, 10/16/85 A.M., p. 44.

3. Gregor Sambor, MOVE Commission Hearings, 10/17/85 A.M., p. 157.

4. Poovey, *Uneven Developments*, p. 19.

5. Gregor Sambor, MOVE Commission Hearings, 10/17/85 P.M., pp. 24–25.

6. Bakhtin, *The Dialogic Imagination*, p. 305.

7. Bogen and Lynch, "Taking Account of the Hostile Native," p. 197.

8. Conley and O'Barr, *Rules versus Relationships*, p. 18.

9. Susan Wells, "Narrative Figures and Subtle Persuasions: The Rhetoric of the MOVE Report," in Simons, *The Rhetorical Turn*, p. 212.

BIBLIOGRAPHY

Aberbach, Joel D., Robert D. Putnam, and Bert A. Rockman. 1981. *Bureaucrats and Politicians in Western Democracies*. Cambridge: Harvard University Press.

American Friends Service Committee. 1986. *Voices from the Community*. Philadelphia: AFSC National Community Relations Committee.

———. 1987. *Reflections One Year Later: An Addendum to Voices from the Community*.

Anderson, Elijah. 1991. *Streetwise*. Chicago: University of Chicago Press.

Anderson, John, and Hilary Hevenor. 1987. *Burning Down the House: MOVE and the Tragedy of Philadelphia*. New York: W. W. Norton and Company.

Arendt, Hannah. 1958. *The Human Condition*. Chicago: University of Chicago Press.

———. 1963. *Eichmann in Jerusalem: A Report on the Banality of Evil*. New York: Viking Press.

Ariès, Philippe. 1962. *Centuries of Childhood*. New York: Vintage Press.

Assefa, Hizkias, and Paul Wahrhaftig. 1988. *Extremist Groups and Conflict Resolution: The MOVE Crisis in Philadelphia*. New York: Praeger.

Bakhtin, M. M. 1981. *The Dialogic Imagination*. Ed. Michael Holquist. Translated by Caryl Emerson and Michael Holquist. Austin: University of Texas Press.

———. 1986. *Speech Genres and Other Late Essays*. Ed. Caryl Emerson and Michael Holquist. Translated by Vern W. McGee. Austin: University of Texas Press.

Bellingham, Bruce. 1983. "The Unspeakable Blessing: Street Children, Reform Rhetoric, and Misery in Early Industrial Capitalism." *Politics and Society* 12, no. 3, pp. 303–30.

Bennett, James. 1981. *Oral History and Delinquency: The Rhetoric of Criminology*. Chicago: University of Chicago Press.

Blau, Peter M. 1968. "The Study of Formal Organization." in *American Sociology: Perspectives, Problems, Methods*, ed. Talcott Parsons, pp. 54–65. New York: Basic Books.

Boden, Deirdre, and Donald Zimmerman, eds. 1991. *Talk and Social Structure*. Berkeley: University of California Press.

Bogen, David, and Michael Lynch. 1989. "Taking Account of the Hostile Native: Plausible Deniability and the Production of Conventional History in the Iran-Contra Hearings." *Social Problems* 36, no. 3, pp. 197–224.

Bourdieu, Pierre. 1987. *Distinction: A Social Critique of the Judgement of Taste.* Cambridge: Harvard University Press.

Bowser, Charles W. 1986. "The Philadelphia Special Investigation Commission, Opinion of Commissioner Charles W. Bowser, Esquire." *Temple Law Quarterly* 51, no. 2.

———. 1988. *Let the Bunker Burn: The Final Battle with MOVE.* Philadelphia: Camino Books.

Boyette, Michael, and Randi Boyette. 1989. "*Let It Burn*": *The Philadelphia Tragedy.* Chicago: Contemporary Books.

Bracy, LaVon Wright, 1990. *Making Them Whole: A Philadelphia Neighborhood and the City's Recovery from the MOVE Tragedy.* Philadelphia: Affie Enterprises.

Brannigan, Augustine, and Michael Lynch. 1987. "On Bearing False Witness: Credibility as an Interactional Accomplishment." *Journal of Contemporary Ethnography* 16, no. 1, pp. 115–46.

Brooks, Peter. 1976. *The Melodramatic Imagination.* New Haven: Yale University Press.

Brown, Gillian, and George Yule. 1985. *Discourse Analysis.* Cambridge: Cambridge University Press.

Brown, Richard. 1981. *Society as Text.* Chicago: University of Chicago Press.

Brown, William, III. 1986. "Foreward to the Report of the Philadelphia Special Investigation Commission." *Temple Law Quarterly* 59, no. 2, pp. 267–69.

Burke, Kenneth. 1969. *A Grammar of Motives.* Berkeley: University of California Press.

Camus, Albert. 1967. *Les Justes.* Paris: Gallimard.

Capuzzo, Michael. 1988. "The Miracle of Birdie Africa." *Philadelphia Inquirer Sunday Magazine,* May 8, pp. 12–21, 28–30.

Cleaver, Kathleen Neal. 1991. "Philadelphia Fire." *Transition,* no. 51, May, pp. 150–57.

Cohen, Stanley. 1985. *Visions of Social Control: Crime, Punishment, and Classification.* Cambridge: Polity Press.

Cohn, Carol. 1987. "Sex and Death in the Rational World of Defense Intellectuals." *Signs* 12, no. 4, pp. 687–718.

Collins, Randall. 1974. "Three Faces of Cruelty: Towards a Comparative Sociology of Violence." *Theory and Society* 1, pp. 415–40.

Conley, John M., and William M. O'Barr. 1990. *Rules versus Relationships: The Ethnography of Legal Discourse.* Chicago: University of Chicago Press.

Coulthard, Malcolm. 1985. *An Introduction to Discourse Analysis.* London: Longman Group.

Cover, Robert M. 1986. "Violence and the Word." *Yale Law Journal* 95, pp. 1601–29.

Cox, Sharon Sims. 1985. "My Life in MOVE" (as told to Carol Saline). *Philadelphia Magazine*, September, pp. 170–72.

Danet, Brenda. 1980. "Language in the Legal Process." *Law and Society Review* 14, no. 3, pp. 445–564.

Danet, Brenda, Kenneth B. Hoffman, and Nicole C. Kermish. 1980. "Threats to the Life of the President: An Analysis of Linguistic Issues." *Journal of Media Law and Practice*, 1, pp. 180–90.

de Certeau, Michel. 1988. *The Practice of Everyday Life*. Translated by Steven Rendall. Berkeley: University of California Press.

Dentith, Simon. 1983. "Political Economy, Fiction, and the Language of Practical Ideology in Nineteenth-Century England." *Social History* no. 2, pp. 183–99.

Dreyfus, Hubert L., and Paul Rabinow. 1983. *Michel Foucault: Beyond Stucturalism and Hermeneutics*. Chicago: University of Chicago Press.

Dunstan, Robert. 1980. "Context for Coercion: Analyzing Properties of Courtroom 'Questions.'" *British Journal of Law and Society* 7, pp. 6–77.

Edelman, Murray. 1988. *Constructing the Political Spectacle*. Chicago: University of Chicago Press.

Elliot, Philip, Graham Murdock, and Philip Schlesinger. 1986. "Terrorism and the State: A Case Study of the Discourses of Television." In *Media, Culture, and Society: A Critical Reader*, eds. Richard Collins et al., pp. 264–86. London: Sage Publications.

Ericson, Richard V., and Clifford D. Shearing. 1986. "The Scientification of Police Work." In *The Knowledge Society*, eds. Gernot Bohme and Nico Stehr, pp. 129–59, Norwell, Mass.: D. Reidel Publisher.

Ermer, Virginia, and John H. Strange, eds. 1972. *Blacks and Bureaucracy: Readings in the Problems and Politics of Change*. New York: Thomas Y. Crowell.

Ervin-Tripp, Susan. 1972. "On Sociolinguistic Rules: Alternation and Co-occurrence." In *Directions in Sociolinguistics: The Ethnography of Communication*, eds. John Gumperz anbd Dell Hymes, pp. 213–50. New York: Holt, Rinehart and Winston.

Ewald, François. 1990. "Norms, Discipline, and the Law." *Representations* 30 (Spring), pp. 138–61.

Feldman, Heidi. 1987. *The MOVE Crisis: A Case Study in Community Conflict*. Senior thesis, Swarthmore College.

Felstiner, William L. F., Richard Abel, and Austin Sarat. 1980–81. "The Emergence and Transformation of Disputes: Naming, Blaming, and Claiming . . ." *Law and Society Review*, 15, nos. 3–4, pp. 631–54.

Ferguson, Kathy E. 1984. *The Feminist Case against Bureaucracy*. Philadelphia: Temple University Press.

Fields, Barbara Jeanne. 1990. "Slavery, Race, and Ideology in the United States of America." *New Left Review*, May–June, pp. 95–118.

The Findings, Conclusions and Recommendations of the Philadelphia Special Investigation Commission. 1986. Philadelphia.

Fisher, Philip. 1985. *Hard Facts: Setting and Form in the American Novel*. New York: Oxford University Press.

Fisher, Susan, and Alexandra Todd, eds. 1986. *Discourse and Institutional*

Authority: Medicine, Education, and Law. Norwood, N.J.: Ablex Publishing.

Foucault, Michel. 1980. *Power/Knowledge.* Ed. Colin Gordon. New York: Pantheon.

Fowler, Roger. 1985. "Power." In *Handbook of Discourse Analysis,* ed. Teun van Dijk, vol. 4, pp. 61–82. London: Academic Press.

Frank, Arthur W., III. 1976. "Making Scenes in Public: Symbolic Violence and Social Order." *Theory and Society* 3, no. 3, pp. 395–416.

Frug, Gerald E. 1984. "The Ideology of Bureaucracy in American Law." *Harvard Law Review* 97, pp. 1276–1388.

Garfinkle, Harold. 1962. *Studies in Ethnomethodology.* Englewood Cliffs, N.J.: Prentice Hall.

Geertz, Clifford. 1973. *The Interpretation of Cultures.* New York: Basic Books.

Goffman, Erving. 1963. *Stigma: Notes on the Management of Spoiled Identity.* Englewood Cliffs, N.J.: Prentice Hall.

———. 1974. *Frame Analysis.* New York: Harper.

Goode, W. Wilson. 1992. *In Goode Faith.* Valley Forge: Pa.: Judson Press.

Goodrich, Peter. 1987. *Legal Discourse: Studies in Linguistics, Rhetoric, and Legal Analysis.* New York: St. Martin's Press.

Grayson, Martin. 1986–87. "The Warrant Clause in Historical Context." *American Journal of Criminal Law* 14, (Fall–Winter), pp. 107–22.

Grillo, Ralph, ed. 1989. *Social Anthropology and the Politics of Language.* London: Routledge.

Grimshaw, Allen, ed. 1990. *Conflict Talk: Sociolinguistic Investigations of Arguments in Conversations.* New York: Cambridge University Press.

Griswold, Wendy. 1987. "A Methodological Framework for the Sociology of Culture." In *Sociological Methodology,* ed. Clifford Clogg, vol. 17, pp. 1–35. Washington, D.C.: American Sociological Association.

Gumperz, John, and Dell Hymes. 1972. *Directions in Sociolinguistics: The Ethnography of Communication.* New York: Holt, Rinehart, and Winston.

Halle, David. 1984. *America's Working Man: Work, Home, and Politics among Blue-Collar Property Owners.* Chicago: University of Chicago Press.

Handler, Joel. 1986. *The Conditions of Discretion: Autonomy, Community, Bureaucracy.* New York: Russell Sage Foundation.

Henriques, Julian, Wendy Hollway, Cathy Urwin, Couze Venn, and Valerie Walkerdine, eds. 1984. *Changing the Subject: Psychology, Social Regulation, and Subjectivity.* London and New York: Methuen.

Herman, Edward. 1982. *The Real Terror Network.* Boston: South End Press.

Jameson, Frederic. 1981. *The Political Unconscious: Narrative as a Socially Symbolic Act.* Ithaca: Cornell University Press.

Karnig, Albert, and Susan Welch. 1980. *Black Representation and Urban Policy.* Chicago: University of Chicago Press.

Keiser, Richard A. 1990. "The Rise of a Biracial Coalition in Philadelphia." In *Racial Politics and American Cities.* eds. Rufus Browning, Dale Marshall, and David Tabb, pp. 49–74. New York: Longman.

Kidder, Robert L. 1980–81. "The End of the Road? Problems in the Analysis of Disputes." *Law and Society Review* 15, nos. 3–4, pp. 717–25.

Kochman, Thomas. 1975. "Orality and Literacy as Factors of 'Black' and 'White' Communicative Behavior." *International Journal of the Sociology of Language,* 3, pp. 95–118.

"Language as Violence v. Freedom of Expression: Canadian and American Perspectives on Group Defamation." *Buffalo Law Review* 37, no. 2 (Spring), pp. 337–73.

LaRue, Lewis. 1988. *Political Discourse: A Case Study of the Watergate Affair.* Athens: University of Georgia Press.

Lerman, Clair L. 1983. "Dominant Discourse: The Institutional Voice and Control of Topic." In *Language, Image, Media,* ed. Howard Davis and Paul Walton, pp. 75–103. New York: St. Martin's Press.

Levine, Donald. 1985. *The Flight from Ambiguity: Essays in Social and Cultural Theory.* Chicago: University of Chicago Press.

Lobelson, Jeanne N. 1989. "The Warrant Clause." *American Criminal Law Review* 26, pp. 2433–56.

Lumley, Robert, and Philip Schlesinger. 1982. "The Press, the State, and Its Enemies: The Italian Case." *Sociological Review,* 30, no. 4, pp. 603–26.

Lyotard, Jean-François. 1984. *The Postmodern Condition: A Report on Knowledge.* Minneapolis: University of Minnesota Press.

MacAloon, John J. 1990. "Steroids and the State: Dubin, Melodrama, and the Accomplishment of Innocence." *Public Culture* 2, no. 1, pp. 41–64.

McCoy, Craig, R. 1986. "Who Was John Africa?" *Philadelphia Inquirer, Sunday Magazine,* January 12, pp. 18–23.

Manning, Peter K. 1989. "On the Phenomenology of Violence." *Criminologist* 14, no. 4 (July–August), pp. 1:4–6:22.

———. 1990. "The Police." In *Handbook of Contemporary Criminology,* pp. 1–49. Belmont, Calif.: Wadsworth Press.

Marx, Gary. 1988. *Undercover: Police Survillance in America.* Berkeley: University of California Press.

Mather, Lynn, and Barbara Yngvesson. 1980–81. "Language, Audience, and the Transformation of Disputes." *Law and Society Review* 15, nos. 3–4, pp. 775–821.

Molotch, Harvey, and Deirdre Boden. 1985. "Talking Social Structure: Discourse, Domination, and the Watergate Hearings." *American Sociological Review* 50, pp. 273–88.

MOVE. 1992. *Twenty Years on the MOVE.* Philadelphia.

Nagel, Jack H. 1991. "Psychological Obstacles to Administrative Responsibility: Lessons of the MOVE Disaster." *Journal of Policy Analysis and Management* 10, no. 1, pp. 1–23.

Nedelsky, Jennifer. 1991. "Laws, Boundaries, and the Bounded Self." In *Law and the Order of Culture,* ed. and intro. Robert Post, pp. 162–189. Berkeley: University of California Press.

O'Barr, William M. 1981. "The Language of the Law." In *Language in the U.S.A.,* ed. Charles Ferguson and Shirley Heath, pp. 386–406. Cambridge: Cambridge University Press.

Philadelphia Special Investigation Commission Records. 1988. Urban Archives Collection, Temple University, Philadelphia.

Platt, Anthony M. ed. 1971. *The Politics of Riot Commission, 1917–1970.* New York: Macmillan Company.

Poovey, Mary. 1988. *Uneven Developments: The Ideological Work of Gender in Mid-Victorian England.* Chicago: University of Chicago Press.

Pratt, Mary Louise. 1987. "Linguistic Utopias." In *The Linguistics of Writing,* ed. Nigel Falb, pp. 48–66. New York: Methuen.

Rapport, Nigel. 1987. *Talking Violence: An Anthropological Interpretation or Conversation in the City.* St. Johns, Newfoundland: Institute of Social and Economic Research.

Reider, Jon. 1985. *Canarsie: The Jews and Italians of Brooklyn against Liberalism.* Cambridge: Harvard University Press.

Rubenstein, Richard. 1987. *Alchemists of Revolution: Terrorism in the Modern World.* New York: Basic Books.

Rubinstein, Jonathan. 1971. *City Police.* New York: Farrar, Strauss, and Company.

Sacks, Harvey. 1984. "On Doing 'Being Ordinary.'" In *Structures of Social Action: Studies in Conversational Analysis,* ed. Maxwell Atkinson and John Heritage, pp. 216–32. Cambridge: Cambridge University Press.

Sacks, Harvey, Emanual A. Schegloff, and Gail Jefferson. 1974. "A Simplest Systematics for the Organization of Turn-taking in Conversation." *Language* 50, pp. 696–735.

Sanchez-Eppler, Karen. 1988. "Bodily Bonds: The Intersecting Rhetorics of Feminism and Abolition." *Representations* 24 (Fall) pp. 28–59.

Scarry, Elaine. 1985. *The Body in Pain.* New York: Oxford University Press.

Scott, Marvin, and Stanford Lyman. 1968. "Accounts." *American Sociological Review* 33, no. 1, pp. 46–62.

Shklar, Judith N. 1986. *Legalism: Law, Morals, and Political Trials.* Cambridge: Harvard University Press.

Simons, Herbert H. ed. 1990. *The Rhetorical Turn: Invention and Persuasion in the Conduct of Inquiry.* Chicago: University of Chicago Press.

de Sousa Santos, Boaventura. 1977. "The Law of the Oppressed: The Construction and Reproduction of Legality in Pasargarda." *Law and Society Review* 12.

Stallybrass, Peter. 1990. "Marx and Heterogeneity: Thinking the Lumpenproletariat." *Representations,* no. 31 (Summer), pp. 69–95.

Stern, Paul G. 1990. "A Pluralistic Reading of the First Amendment and Its Relation to Public Discourse." *Yale Law Journal* 99, pp. 925–44.

Sutton, Paul. 1986. "The Fourth Amendment in Action: An Empirical View of the Search Warrant Process." *Criminal Law Bulletin* 22, pp. 405–429.

Swett, Daniel H. 1969. "Cultural Bias in the American Legal System." *Law and Society Review,* no. 1, pp. 79–110.

Tompkins, Jane. 1985. *Sentimental Designs: The Cultural Work of American Fiction, 1790–1860.* Oxford: Oxford University Press.

Turner, Roy, ed. 1974. *Ethnomethodology.* Harmondsowrth: Penguin Education.

Urban League of Philadelphia. 1985. *The State of Black Philadelphia*. Philadelphia: Urban League of Philadelphia.

van Dijk, Teun. 1985. *Handbook of Discourse Analysis*. 4 vols. London: Academic Press.

Van Maanen, John. 1983. "The Moral Fix: On the Ethics of Fieldwork." In *Contemporary Field Research*, ed. Robert M. Emerson. Boston: Little, Brown.

Vidich, Arthur J., and Joseph Bensman. 1968. *Small Town in Mass Society. Class, Power, and Religion in a Rural Community*. Garden City, N.Y.: Doubleday.

Wagner-Pacifici, Robin. 1986. *The Moro Morality Play: Terrorism as Social Drama*. Chicago: University of Chicago Press.

Wagner-Pacifici, Robin, and Barry Schwartz. 1991. "The Vietnam Veterans Memorial: Commemorating a Difficult Past." *American Journal of Sociology* 97, no. 2, pp. 376–420.

Weber, Max. 1958. *From Max Weber: Essays in Sociology*. Translated and ed. Hans Gerth and C. Wright Mills. New York: Oxford University Press.

White, Hayden. 1973. *Metahistory: The Historical Imagination in the Nineteenth Century*. Baltimore: Johns Hopkins University Press.

Wideman, John Edgar. 1990. *Philadelphia Fire*. New York: Holt.

Wilson, William Julius. 1987. *The Truly Disadvantaged*. Chicago: University of Chicago Press.

Wooton, Anthony. 1975. *Dilemmas of Discourse*. New York: Holmes and Meier Publishers.

Zelizer, Viviana. 1985. *Pricing the Priceless Child*. New York: Basic Books.

INDEX